Critical Guides to French Texts

GW00374879

Critical Guides to French Texts

EDITED BY ROGER LITTLE, WOLFGANG VAN EMDEN, DAVID WILLIAMS

VOLTAIRE

Candide

David Williams

Professor of French in the University of Sheffield

Grant & Cutler Ltd
1997

© Grant & Cutler Ltd 1997

ISBN 0 7293 0395 0

DEPÓSITO LEGAL: V. 1.056 - 1997

Printed in Spain by
Artes Gráficas Soler, S.A., Valencia
for
GRANT & CUTLER LTD
55–57 GREAT MARLBOROUGH ST, LONDON W1V 2AY

Contents

for Richard and Tor

References

References to the text of *Candide* are to the edition by Jacques Popin (Paris, Bordas, 1994). This edition reproduces the text printed in the last edition of Voltaire's works authorised by Voltaire (the 1775 Cramer 'encadrée'), but with modernised spelling and punctuation. Reference is in parenthesis by chapter number followed by line number(s) separated by a colon.

References to other works by Voltaire are either to the new collective edition of Voltaire's works still in progress (*1*), or to the Moland edition (*2*). References to Voltaire's correspondence are to the second, definitive Besterman edition (*3*), letters being identified by the prefix D followed by the letter number in arabic.

All other references, indicated in parenthesis by italicised arabic numerals, are to the numbered items in the Select Bibliography.

For valuable advice and help, I am indebted to Professor Haydn Mason.

1. Note on Composition and Publication

Voltaire offers few clues to the composition of his most celebrated *conte*. His correspondence is silent as far as specific indications of when, or why, he started writing *Candide*. We must wait until after the *conte*'s publication to find a reference in a letter to a friend in February 1759 to 'je ne sais quel *Candide*' (D8119), and then it was only to deny authorship (*11*, pp.9-10).

Composition probably started in the autumn of 1757, and continued through the winter months of 1757-1758 when Voltaire was living in Lausanne (*7*, p.31). On 1 July 1758 Voltaire left Lausanne for Mannheim and Schwetzingen, and he took a sketch of *Candide* with him for use as a working script for the entertainment of the court of Karl Theodor, the Elector of the Palatine. Work on the *conte* itself was still far from finished when Voltaire left Schwetzingen some six weeks later.

The next phase of composition started after the visit of Charlotte-Sophia, Countess Bentinck, to Geneva in the late summer of 1758. She was a Westphalian aristocrat, and Voltaire's letters to her before and after her visit certainly contain many echoes of the text of *Candide*. The first draft was ready soon after the Countess's departure in September/October 1758, and the manuscript was sent to the duc de La Vallière in Paris in the autumn of 1758 (*39*, pp.157-58).

A further polishing took place between the end of October and mid-December. Voltaire now made important revisions to the La Vallière manuscript, adding the negro slave episode in Chapter 19, probably after having read the section on slavery in Helvétius's *De l'esprit* (a copy of which he had received in October), the attribution on the title-page to 'Dr Ralph', certain obfuscating modifications to the allusions to Robert Damiens's attempted assassination of Louis XV in 1757 in the Paris scenes in Chapter 22, and other changes (*13*, pp.49-72). The text of the first edition was ready by December 1758 (*7*, pp.53-62). Further alterations were made in 1761, but after 1761 there were no more major revisions.

Because it was such an incandescently dangerous work, publication had to be carefully managed, the penalties for unauthorised publications being severe. The measures taken to ensure the successful dissemination of what was called in a contemporary police report 'une mauvaise plaisanterie sur tous les pays et tous les peuples' (*39*, p.188) have made it difficult to establish the exact date of publication. *Candide* emerged unheralded from the presses of Voltaire's Genevan publisher, Gabriel Cramer, sometime in mid-January 1759 in an initial print-run of 2,000 copies. Unbound copies (easier to smuggle) were dispatched from Geneva on 15 and 16 January to Paris and other capitals, publication taking place simultaneously in five countries.

By 22 February more than a thousand copies were circulating in Paris without permission. The Council of Geneva noted *Candide*'s silent appearance on 23 February, and the *conte* was denounced officially in France the following day. In Paris copies were seized by the police, and the presses printing extra copies smashed. *Candide* proved unstoppable, however. Six thousand copies in six editions had sold in Paris by 10 March, and 200,000 copies outside France. John Nourse's English translation, *Candid, or All for Best*, as well as two other English translations, appeared in the same year, as well as an Italian translation. Before the end of 1759 seventeen French editions are known to have been published (*7*, pp.53-64), and over fifty appeared during Voltaire's lifetime. Although publication had taken place anonymously, Voltaire's name soon featured in police reports, and he was publicly named as 'M. de Volt.' in an unauthorised edition in 1759. Voltaire himself did not acknowledge authorship openly until 1768.

In eighteenth-century terms, *Candide* was an immediate best-seller, its sales fortified no doubt by its fierce condemnation as a work harmful to religion and morally depraving. It was placed on the Index of Forbidden Books in 1762. *Candide* was, in other words, a stunning success.

2. The Cruel Philosophy

Candide's subtitle is '*ou l'optimisme*', but the allusion is not to optimism in the accepted modern sense indicating simply a positive, looking-on-the-bright-side approach to life, but to Optimism, that is to say, to a philosophical system peculiar to late seventeenth- and mid-eighteenth-century theological disputation. In *Candide* Voltaire aimed to seize Optimism by the throat, satirically speaking, and destroy its credibility as a way of thinking capable of addressing usefully the grim facts of the human condition. Behind the caricatural reduction of Optimistic theory to the well-known Panglossian slogan 'tout est au mieux', lie echoes of a long-running and complex dispute between philosophers and theologians relating to the problem of evil, still being hotly debated in educated circles when Voltaire was writing *Candide* (*11*, pp.41-49). Optimism in fact continued to fuel philosophical debate and to fire the imagination of writers well after *Candide* (*10*, p.41), as can be seen in the story of Dr Primrose in Oliver Goldsmith's *The Vicar of Wakefield* (1766). Its reverberations continued into the next century with Musset and Vigny, and into our own with the work of Camus and Beckett.

The debate started in an exchange of views between Pierre Bayle and an archbishop of Dublin, William King. In the entry 'Rorarius' in his controversial *Dictionnaire historique et philosophique* (1697), and also in his *Réponse aux questions d'un provincial* (1701-1703), Bayle had doubted the capacity of any philosophical, reason-based system to resolve the mysterious paradox arising from the coexistence of human suffering with divine goodness and omnipotence. Bayle saw an irreconcilable duality at the heart of creation, although he never went as far as the Manicheans in envisaging the possibility of the ultimate triumph of evil over good. Voltaire's admiration for Bayle's anti-systems stance (*24*, pp.30, 36) is reflected in the *Poème sur le désastre de Lisbonne* (1756), composed after the great earthquake struck Lisbon (and Seville, Cadiz and several other cities) in 1755. In 1702 King countered Bayle's agnosticism in *De origine mali,* arguing the case for the necessary existence of evil as an indispensable component of the general good.

A key element of Optimism was now in place, and after Bayle's death in 1706, the evolution of Optimistic theory continued with the work of thinkers like Bernard and Jacquelot, culminating in 1710 in the *Essais de théodicée sur la bonté de Dieu, la liberté de l'homme et l'origine du mal,* published in French by a German philosopher named Gottfried Leibniz.

Leibniz's *Théodicée* is a substantial, sophisticated treatise combining investigations into physics as well as metaphysics. It addressed the two issues rehearsed by Bayle and King: first, the problem of man's freedom, a notion seemingly incompatible with belief in an omniscient and omnipotent God, but indispensable if man is to bear moral responsibility for his actions; secondly, the question of God's benevolence, given His admission of evil into creation. Leibnizian Optimism sought to demonstrate not that the world is a perfect place, but that in creating the world God, an infinitely wise and benevolent 'première raison des choses', could out of logical necessity only have created the best world possible, having reviewed through time and space all the potential models, and weighed up the 'compossibles'.

From His infinite understanding of the possibilities, the world as we know it came into existence – an *optimum* of logic and rationality, subsuming evil as a regrettable, but necessary, part of the natural order, everything in creation existing in a certain form, and no other, within optimal parameters. The reality of evil was not denied in absolute terms, but through the *raison suffisante* argument Leibniz offered a view of the cosmos as a rational *enchaînement* of causes and effects accounting

morally and rationally for evil as an integral link in a Great
Chain of Being without compromising orthodox views of God's
nature. Philosophical ratiocination, despised and dismissed as
absurd 'raisonnements' in *Candide*, was for Leibniz and his
eighteenth-century successors an effective tool for making sense
of the world.

Leibniz died in 1716. The Leibnizian baton was picked
up by another German thinker, Christian-Friedrich Wolff.
Wolff, a professor of philosophy at the University of Halle, was
the author of a series of works, including the *Logique* (1728-36),
the *Ontologie* (1730), the *Cosmologie* (1731), the *Psychologie
expérimentale et rationnelle* (1732-34) and the *Théologie naturelle*
(1736). Mocking echoes of these titles can be detected in
Chapter 1 of *Candide* where we learn that Dr Pangloss, who at
the end of the tale is still 'au désespoir de ne pas briller dans
quelque université d'Allemagne' (30:26-27), teaches 'métaphysico-théologo-cosmolonigologie' (1:27). A Wolffian/Pan-
glossian cosmology is a system designed to encompass a vision
of the mysteries of nature and of the human condition within a
single, unifying, scientifically coherent principle that would
account for 'tout'. 'Tout' appears in the subtitle to Voltaire's
Poème sur le désastre de Lisbonne, and the volatile word occupies
a central position in *Candide*'s symbolic codes (*10*, pp.34-35).

In his re-interpretation of the cosmology of Leibniz's
Théodicée Wolff aimed to turn Leibizian Optimism into a
scientifically rigorous demonstration of the truths of the
Christian faith whose power as a system could be released
through mathematics. It is no coincidence that numbers and
statistics play an important role in Voltaire's send-up of all this
in *Candide*, and anti-Wolffian aspects of the tale imbue Dr
Pangloss with many of his distinguishing features. Wolff died in
1754 at the height of his international reputation, but
Leibnizio-Wolffism was still very much in the air throughout
the 1750s, its cause being further disseminated by Jean-Henri-
Samuel Formey in his influential vulgarisation, *La Belle
Wolffienne* (1760).

Voltaire also sought to undermine a refinement of Optimism, developed by English philosophers, such as Bolingbroke and Shaftesbury, called Providentialism, of which the best-known formulation, Alexander Pope's *Essay on Man* (1733), was translated into French by Voltaire in 1737-38. The emphasis in Pope's poem was on the consolation to be derived from an awareness of the continuing presence of God in nature, and of the over-arching principle of good in creation:

Cease then, nor ORDER imperfection name:
Our proper bliss depends on what we blame [...].
All Nature is but Art, unknown to thee;
All Chance, Direction, which thou canst not see;
All Discord, Harmony, not understood;
All partial Evil, universal Good.
And, spite of Pride, in erring Reason's spite,
One truth is clear, 'Whatever IS, is RIGHT'.

By the early 1750s Voltaire was convinced that Optimism was a system of thought whose crushing fatalism paralysed man's will to act, and denied all possibility of change and progress. Soon after the Lisbon earthquake, he wrote to Tronchin: 'Voylà monsieur une phisique bien cruelle. On sera bien embarassé à deviner comment les loix du mouvement opèrent des désastres si effroiables dans le *meilleur des mondes possibles*' (D6597). In discounting the realities of evil as 'Harmony, not understood', the Optimists were distorters of a central fact of human existence whose truth was not to be denied: 'Le mal est sur la terre, et c'est se moquer de moi que de dire que mille infortunez composent le bonheur [...]. L'optimisme est désespérant. C'est une philosofie cruelle sous un nom consolant' (D6738).

Voltaire's stance against Pope in *Candide* is discreet. Pope is never mentioned by name, and indeed Leibniz is mentioned specifically only once (28:80). Voltaire admired the *Essay on Man* as a poem, and in the preface to the *Poème sur le désastre de*

Lisbonne Pope was deemed less 'enragé' than the German Optimists. As a result, the Optimism targeted in *Candide* has Germanic colours.

Three years separate *Candide* from the *Poème sur le désastre de Lisbonne*, and the relevance of Voltaire's powerfully emotive poetic response to the Optimists in the light of the Lisbon catastrophe to *Candide* should not be overstated. The *Poème* is not the prelude to *Candide*, which was written in a very different mood, but it does illuminate the symbolic code of the *conte*, the earthquake itself providing one of the tale's major scenarios. The challenge to Pangloss and to Optimism in Chapter 5, for example, is already in place in the *Poème*:

> Philosophes trompés qui criez 'Tout est bien',
> Accourez, contemplez ces ruines affreuses.
> Ces débris, ces lambeaux, ces cendres malheureuses.

In *Candide* Pangloss would play the role of the cold philosopher-spectator of the *Poème*, distanced by a cruel system from the horrors of the ruined city, from the suffering of its citizens, and also from his own humanity:

> Tranquilles spectateurs, intrépides esprits,
> De vos frères mourants contemplant les naufrages,
> Vous recherchez en paix les causes des orages.

Here, as in *Candide*, philosophers avert their gaze from the truth, the hard facts of life and death becoming almost invisible as 'partial evils' within a 'universal Good':

> Et vous composez, dans ce chaos fatal,
> Des malheurs de chaque être un bonheur général
> [...]
> Tout est bien, dites-vous, et tout est nécessaire.

In the *Poème* Voltaire challenged the 'tristes calculateurs des misères humaines' to look the victims of Lisbon straight in the eye and not take refuge in philosophical platitudes, a challenge to be taken up by Jean-Jacques Rousseau in his *Lettre sur la providence* (1756), addressed to Voltaire. For Voltaire, however, the assumption that all was for the best was no longer sustainable after the loss of life in Lisbon: 'Voilà un terrible argument contre l'optimisme' (D6605). Experimentation with a fresh, satirical angle of attack came with the publication of a prototypical *Candide* in 1756, the *Histoire des voyages de Scarmentado*.

The *Poème*, however, did open a chink of light in the darkness that would also flicker across *Candide*'s bleak landscape. Man might be just another tormented atom doomed to suffer and die on a heap of mud floating in an indifferent cosmos but man was a thinking atom, with the potential to free himself from illusory systems and acquire true self-knowledge. The light in the *Poème* is the light of hope:

> *Un jour tout sera bien*, voilà notre espérance:
> Tout est bien aujourd'hui, voilà l'illusion.

In the *Poème* hope is a dynamic, empowering force for the future, unique to man, his key to action and freedom, and the most effective response to the crushing constraints of 'le tout'.

We see Optimism recede before a cautious optimism, with its modern, liberating connotations of a projected future to be envisaged through hope and realised through action, leaving behind its metaphysical associations with an *optimum* already in place when the world came into existence. This important reorientation paves the way for the Old Woman's courageous nonchalance and dismissal of life's inexplicable reverses as 'une bagatelle' (11:29) as well as for the glimpse of a better world in Eldorado, 'car il faut [...] qu'il y en ait de cette espèce' (17:115), and the provisional compromise with life as it is that Candide settles for in the end.

The satirical destruction of philosophical Optimism and Providentialism is the original organising principle behind *Candide*, and Voltaire's merciless exposure of the timeless life and death issues involved still resonates powerfully, not least because his attack is not confined to the terms of an arcane philosophical dispute, whose time came and went nearly three hundred years ago. In Dr Pangloss's 'métaphysico-théologo-cosmolonigologie', its slogans repeated with a mechanical rigidity that always triggers laughter, Voltaire parades before us the menacing absurdities of all 'systems' and 'cruel philosophies' that still seek to provide soft answers to complex questions, and induce the sleep of reason.

3. Structure and Dynamics

Voltaire wrote twenty-six short stories, of which eight have stood the test of time. The best, most complex, blackest, and certainly the funniest, is *Candide*, and he took great pains to get it just right. Of all his *contes*, *Candide* is the one with universal, mythical qualities combining withering satire of a particular world-view with an exquisitely stylised parody of the sentimental and picaresque *topoi* of contemporary novels (which he detested) and other narrative traditions such as the chivalric romance, utopic and travel literature, fairy and folk-tale (*25*, pp.83-85; *36*), to say nothing of the 'roman' of theology and metaphysics.

Candide is not a philosophical treatise in disguise (*6*, pp.xlvii-xlviii; *16*, p.102). Nevertheless, Voltaire's assault on Optimism shapes all aspects of his narrative strategy, from imagery and word-play to settings, plot-structure and characterisation. The regularity with which Pangloss's formulaic distillation of Optimism to variations on the slogan 'Tout est pour le mieux dans le meilleur des mondes possibles' has a narrative frequency generating what modern critical theorists like Genette would see as good examples of *récit itératif* by means of which Voltaire deflects the need to engage with the technicalities of Optimistic argument. His concern is not with philosophical niceties but with the implications of the Optimistic approach to life for ordinary people trying to make sense of their lives in a dangerous, hideously absurd world. The carnivalesque spectacle (*21*; *22*, pp.81-95) of human beings struggling for survival and purpose is central to the power of the tale's hypnotic spell. Unlike the *Poème sur le désastre de*

Lisbonne, serious philosophical issues are beneath the surface, obliquely and ironically implied.

At approximately fifteen thousand words, *Candide* is long for a Voltairean *conte*. Half of the thirty chapters have about a thousand words each, and two chapters (23 and 29) contain less than five hundred. Chapter 22, revised and extended in 1761, is the longest, though not the most successful from the standpoint of sustained satirical quality. In mocking imitation of the picaresque style, most chapters are headed by a brief descriptive sub-heading, offering the reader a laconic, anticipatory summation of events to come, which often derides simultaneously the notion of pre-established harmony and design. The title-page informs the reader with significant immediacy after the subtitle, *ou l'optimisme*, that the tale has been translated from a German manuscript found in the pocket of a certain Dr Ralph, killed at the Battle of Minden in 1759.

'Monsieur le Dr Ralph' is the first recorded casualty in the tale. His academic/theological title, shared by one of the key characters in the plot about to unfold, hints that the corpse might be that of another intellectual, a system-builder perhaps. His manuscript has been found, not in the usual attic or desk-drawer of the conventional novel as part of a controlled order of events, but inconsequentially by unexplained chance in lethal, Optimism-denying circumstances. In a letter written on 1 April 1759 over the name of Démad to the *Journal encyclopédique* (D8239), attributing the authorship of *Candide* to an army captain, Voltaire identified Dr Ralph as the captain's collaborator, '[un] professeur assez connu dans l'Académie de Francfort sur l'Oder'. On the title-page this learned German Doctor, together with any system he might have professed, has literally hit the dust in one of the bloodiest battles of the Seven Years' War before the tale starts. In short, the title-page tells us that this is a story 'born of death, determined by chance' (*22*, p.82; cf. *32*, pp.139-40).

There are sixteen changes of location involving thirteen named countries or cities in Candide's journey from Europe to the New World and back again, starting in war-torn Westphalia and ending in Turkey. Settings, none of which are sustained for longer than two chapters, have no role to play in *Candide* other than that required by the thematic considerations. Voltaire does not use settings to explore interaction between character and environment, or to create 'atmosphere' or the illusion of realism, although *Candide* is occasionally disconcertingly realistic. There are ten principals, of whom nine survive. By the time the tale draws to an end, they have lost their national characteristics and allegiances to become unaffiliated human beings (*29*, p.133), an important condition for the success of Candide's garden. They are still 'labelled' characters, however, in accordance with the semic and referential codes that remain operative throughout the narrative: Candide (the eponymous hero, a bastard and Cunégonde's lover), Cunégonde (the tasty daughter of the Baron and Baroness Thunder-ten-Tronckh), the Baron's son (later to become a Jesuit and in due course the new Baron), Dr Pangloss (an Optimist and first of Candide's mentors), Paquette (the Baroness's chamber-maid and later a prostitute), Jacques (a Dutch Anabaptist and businessman), Martin (a Manichean), Cacambo (Candide's servant in later stages of the tale), the Old Woman (once a princess but now Cunégonde's companion/servant), Giroflée (an unhappy *théatin* monk and Paquette's companion/lover). Only two are designated as philosophers, Pangloss and Martin, and neither is a guarantor of truth and wisdom, although the latter is more sympathetically drawn than the former, and is blessed with more good sense. Candide trembles like a philosopher in Chapter 3 (3:10), and is counted temporarily as a philosopher in Chapter 4 (4:85).

There is in addition a chorus of secondary characters of varying importance identified by name or title, often reflecting stereotypical racial and national traits (*29*, pp.132-33): Baron Thunder-ten-Tronckh and his substantial Baroness, the King of the Bulgars, Don Issacar, the Grand Inquisitor, the Governor of Buenos Aires, the King of Eldorado, M. Vanderdendur,

Mme de Parolignac, Pococuranté, four of the Six Kings, Sultan
Achmet III, Ivan (Emperor of Russia), Charles-Edouard (the
Young Pretender) and Théodore (King of Corsica). Many
anonymous, but individually drawn, secondary characters have
significant thematic functions: the recruiting sergeants, the
Dutch preacher and his wife, the vicious sailor, the two *Oreillon*
girls and their monkey-lovers, the Eldoradan *bon vieillard,* the
negro slave, the *abbé périgourdin,* a Parisian wit, an English
admiral, a *levanti patron,* a dervish and a Turkish farmer.

There are in addition allusions to contemporaries such as
Adrienne Lecouvreur, a much admired actress-friend denied a
Christian burial because of her profession and thinly disguised
as Mlle Monime, and enemies such as Fréron ('un F'), Trublet
('l'archidiacre T'), Gauchat, Maupertuis ('un savant du nord'),
and an obscure political celebrity of the time, Prince Ragotski
of Transylvania. There is a dangerous passing reference to
Louis XV's would-be assassin, Damiens ('un gueux du pays
d'Atrébatie'). The English admiral executed in Portsmouth
harbour is John Byng, commanding admiral of the losing side
in the naval battle against the French at Minorca in 1758, for
whom Voltaire had in fact tried to intercede. The tale's
referential code, involving the use of real contemporaries as
'characters' in the grip of real events, anchors parts of the plot
to a vivid historicity quite alien to the traditions of the genre.

Candide also teems with crowds and groups of
undifferentiated characters that give the tale much of its vitality
as spectators of executions and burnings, raging lynch-mobs,
crowds in the various tavern scenes, gamblers and brothel
frequenters, theatre-goers and *salonniers,* Jesuit *colons,*
Paraguayan primitives, Eldoradans, children, inn-keepers,
soldiers, priests, guards, servants and courtiers. Some crowds
generate a powerfully emotive impact as mute but eloquent
heaps of dead and wounded on the battlefields of Westphalia
and Morocco, looted corpses in the ruins of Lisbon, drowning
victims of sea disasters, or simply as statistics on the death-toll
of killer-diseases. All are brushed in with consummate skill,

their entrances and exits carefully managed, and their place in the overall satirical design carefully calculated. Candide is present, actively or passively, in every chapter. Martin appears in twelve, Cacambo and the Old Woman in eleven, and Cunégonde in ten. Pangloss is present throughout by allusion, usually through Candide, although he makes an appearance in only seven chapters.

Voltaire's authorial stance is technically that of 'translator' of the Ralph manuscript. In fact, he adopts a number of stances: sometimes that of an omniscient narrator, sometimes a neutral witness to events, sometimes narrating through a character. The narratorial *je* appears only once, at the start of the tale (1:5), but is enough to establish an ambiance of collusion between author and reader. This is reinforced periodically by the use of possessive adjectives and pronouns to denote a shared ownership of the narrative: 'nos deux hommes de l'autre monde' (17:50), 'nos deux voyageurs' (19:1), 'que nous nommons *or* et *pierreries*' (18:83). Author-reader complicity is also implied by judgmental designations: 'les deux vagabonds' (18:167), 'notre bon Westphalien' (9:7). It is further consolidated by ironic inflexion in reportage of events, by the transparently artificial manipulation of settings and recognition scenes, the arch quaintness of chapter headings, a knowingly exaggerated use of coincidence and cliffhangers, parataxis and word-play, mechanical repetition, flashbacks, and asides (*16*, pp.163-72).

Authorial guidance is also given to the reader through a generous use of deictic anchors: 'En raisonnant ainsi' (21:50-51), 'La vieille leur parla en ces termes' (10:59-60), 'elle reprit ainsi le fil de son histoire' (8:14), 'mais comment se séparer de Cunégonde, et où se réfugier?' (13:70-71), as well as through the frequent use of 'voilà' and 'voici' (*32*, pp.145-55). Tenses also help to reinforce the reader's complicity by facilitating movement backwards and forwards in the here-and-now of the narrator's (and the reader's) time, by offering a temporary exit from the narrated past of a particular scene in order to direct

the reader's attention to events in the time and space of other
chapters, or to involve the reader in the immediacy of events:
'Les voilà qui se mettent tous deux à table' (8:91). Like all
Voltaire's *contes*, *Candide* was composed on the assumption of
active reader participation (*12*, p.147). It is a testimony to
Voltaire's skills that none of these devices of collusion and
alienation (in the Brechtian sense) reduces the narrative to a
crudely schematic mechanicity or, more seriously, to the
demonstration of a pre-established harmony it was intended to
rebut.

Candide works partly also as a *conte de formation* (*29*,
pp.115-19), and four of the major characters function in
different ways and at different times as the hero's mentor, or as
the source of important truths: Cunégonde, Jacques, the Old
Woman, and Cacambo. Pangloss and Martin, from whom a
more formal didactic function might be expected, are in fact
'anti-mentors', sources of misinformation and propounders of
false philosophies. Important contributions to Candide's
education also come from seven secondary characters: the
Eldoradan 'bon vieillard', the King of Eldorado, the negro
slave, Mme de Parolignac, Pococuranté, the dervish and the
Turkish farmer. The 'abbé périgourdin' could be added to this
list, if only as a source of negative education.

Characters in Voltaire's tales, like settings and events, are
often seen as functions of theme, 'symbols, two-dimensional
projections of philosophic fantasy' (*16*, pp.70-71), shadow-
graphs or puppets (*6*, p.xxxix) with little psychological depth
and evolution. Commentators have seen something of a magic
lantern show at work in *Candide*. The 'set-piece' consequences
of this have been noted by many commentators in scenes such
as the lover's first kiss in Chapter 1, the military training scene
in Chapter 2, the battle in Morocco in Chapter 11, the naval
engagement off Surinam in Chapter 20, the salon and
gambling-den scenes in Chapter 22, and the Byng execution in
Chapter 23. It is true that in *Candide* we are not dealing with
the rounded figures of novels, but Voltaire's characters are not

always rudimentary mechanicals or merely mouthpieces for the author. Characters in *Candide* can surprise the reader with a sudden escape from their prescribed roles, Cunégonde, Pangloss and particularly the Old Woman being interesting examples. None is more capable of surprising the reader than Candide himself when he runs Don Issacar through with his sword, and then murders the Grand Inquisitor by repeatedly stabbing him, 'quoiqu'il eût les mœurs fort douces' (9:8-29). Even Cunégonde is shocked by her lover's violence (9:31-33).

Candide first saw the light of day as a court entertainment, a kind of script for voices, and the oral and theatrical qualities of the tale have been retained in a printed text that is still predominantly dialogic. Voltaire enjoyed reading *Candide* aloud to friends, and he exploited fully the satirical potential of sound-effects. Many characters have names with a comic alliteration that tags the essence of their nature or function, and helps to establish a clear semic code, which in some cases has to be revised as the tale unfolds. Candide, from the Latin *candidus*, connotes whiteness, openness, naïvety, innocence and, more negatively, inexperience and credulity. Our view of Candide is not allowed to remain static, however, and later on in the tale other, very different connotations develop.

Cunégonde is a name with multiple historical associations with chastity, piety, and saintliness. Queen Kunigunde, wife of the eleventh century Holy Roman Emperor Heinrich II and patron saint of Bamberg where she lies buried, is still remembered in that city, not least for her ability to walk on hot embers. Her name probably first caught Voltaire's attention during his stay in Potsdam in 1750-53. With echoes of the exotic 'reine de Golconde', celebrated by Boufflers, to French ears it also has an initial syllable that sounds like *cul* while based on the Latin *cunnus* (vagina). Cacambo has a similar scatological echo, with supplementary exotic hints of *cacao*. Pangloss, from the Greek *pan* and *glossa*, is literally 'all mouth' or 'all words', his name incorporating etymologically the dangerous word 'tout'. Thunder-ten-Tronckh reverberates with

hard Germanic consonants evoking the boom and bombast
of dogma and arbitrary power, subverted by its comic phon-
etic impact. Unpronounceably harsh Germanic phonemes
march with clockwork precision through the name of the
Baron's neighbouring village, Valdberghoff-trarbk-dickdorff.
Pococuranté's name tells us that this is a man who cares for
little. Vanderdendur coincides phonetically with *vendeur-dents-
durs*, though in fact it is an amalgam traceable to an Amsterdam
magistrate named Vanderdussen and a Hague bookseller
named Vanduren with whom Voltaire had quarrelled (*6*,
pp.127-28). Paquette (Daisy) might have been taken from La
Fontaine's *Le Curé et la mort* (*7*, pp.237-38), and Giroflée,
another crushed flower, has a vague association with *giflé*. Both
have a pleasing simplicity that contrasts sharply with the
grandiloquence of the Governor of Buenos Aires whose name
spans three lines of text (13:13-15). Parolignac combines *parole*
with *ligneux* ('gueule de bois'?). Voltaire's enemy Fréron enters
the scene alliteratively, preceded by a sentence hissing with
sibilants interspersed with an obscenely suggestive fricative
(22:93-96). Martin, the prophet of doom, was also Voltaire's
nickname for Fréron, and the name might also have reminded
readers of the Martin of French proverbs (*16*, p.177).

The proairetic code of the narrative (the code governing
the reader's construction of the plot) is not so easily deduced
from the formal features of the tale, ordering devices such as
chapter-headings not being that helpful in this regard. *Candide*
is sometimes envisaged as three 'movements' or blocks of text,
the first ending at Chapter 10 with the departure from Cadiz
for Buenos Aires, and the second ending at Chapter 20 with the
start of the return journey from Surinam to Paris. Others prefer
to see only one break in the text, the journey from the castle to
the threshold of Eldorado (Chapters 1-16) being the first
'initiating' movement, with the block of text from the 'garden'
of Eldorado to Candide's garden in Turkey (Chapters 17-30)
as the second movement constituting the resolution.

Barthes's hermeneutic codes can be applied up to a point to break the tale down into narrative components. Visualising the plot in a schematic way linked to thematic developments, to the 'oscillation psychologique' of the hero, or to changes in geographical setting, can be helpful, but any schematic analysis of *Candide* should not imply a logically evolving linearity, or progressive *enchaînement*. It was precisely that sense of providentialist order, even at the level of narrative structure, that Voltaire wished to negate. The deliberate fracturing of the narrative line is particularly noticeable in the stories of the Old Woman, Cunégonde and the Baron's son in Chapters 8, 11-12 and 15 (*13*, pp.73-88) where Voltaire's handling of time with the use of recapitulation, temporal reversal and re-play does not always synchronise with accounts given in the main narrative. The *récit à tiroir* effect presents the reader with different versions of the same 'facts', and often offers a recapitulation of events from different angles, as with Cunégonde's version of the *auto-da-fé* in Lisbon (Chapter 8). This disrupts any linear reading of the text, and helps also to establish a concurrency of narrative events that is particularly important for the angle of vision from which the conclusion should be interpreted. Cunégonde's story offers fresh perspectives that have a close bearing on Chapters 1, 3, 6 and 7. Events, motives and ideas are constantly being re-evaluated in this way as the tale progresses. Even the dead are not always quite as dead as one might think.

This disruption of providentialism at the level of narrative design is accentuated by Voltaire's use of the device of the journey/quest, a departure and an arrival – according to Propp one of the most traditional forms of narrative. The journey, unfolding over twenty-eight chapters, takes Candide westwards towards the dream of Eldorado for about half of the *conte*, and then eastwards towards the realities of the conclusion. Unlike Pangloss, Candide travels well, and the act of travelling, with its implications of displacement and disruption, highlights and counters the purposeless fixity of

Pangloss's world, confronting it with dynamic principles of change and unpredictability in the form of a bewildering, accelerating kaleidoscope of actions and settings (*10*, pp.41-42; *29*, pp.115-16). Candide seems at one level to be undertaking a journey to nowhere, buffeted to and fro by events, at least in the pre-Eldoradan part of the *conte*. At the same time, however, as an empirical experience his journey connotes progress towards knowledge and self-knowledge. In this respect, some commentators have seen the influence of John Locke's *Essay Concerning Human Understanding* (1690), and have cast Candide as a Lockean hero starting his journey at the end of Chapter 1 as a *tabula rasa*, devoid of innate ideas, arriving at the truth through stages of sense-based experience (e.g. *38*, p.82).

Candide is launched into the world as a disturber of *a priori* principles, disrupting the Optimistic stasis, the *optimum*, of the Baron's castle. His ejection from the castle introduces movement and change, signalled by the transition of narrative tense from imperfect to past historic in the seventh paragraph of Chapter 1, opening up new possibilities for action and experience. From now on, Candide will travel through a senseless, but vibrant 'chaos indébrouillable' in which the random and the unpredictable prevail. The journey soon breaks down the reader's expectation of 'necessary' linkage between successive events and experiences and, apart from the Eldoradan interlude, the plot becomes inherently unstable and volatile from the start of Chapter 2 until Chapters 29-30. Settings, even the weather, can change instantaneously, and characters disappear and reappear arbitrarily.

The convolutions of the journey arise at the narrative, though not of course compositional, level, from chance not design, the disorientating effects being at their strongest between Candide's departure from Westphalia and his arrival in Eldorado. After the departure from Eldorado, the quest element in Candide's journey starts to predominate, and the emphasis on displacement and dislocation becomes less dramatic after Candide starts to dispel some of the chaos threatening to engulf him. While his journey will eventually acquire a renewed sense of purpose after Chapter 18, it nevertheless retains its central narrative function throughout the tale as a device to spring surprises on the reader. To get from Paris to Venice will still require Candide to travel first in the opposite direction to Dieppe and Portsmouth.

Narrative momentum is sustained by a number of devices which sharpen the reader's curiosity to know what happens next. Expectations are built up, and suspense raised, with the use of chapter-headings and cliff-hangers, adroit change of tense from past to future in the closing paragraphs of chapters, and authorial intervention – often in the form of tongue-in-cheek rhetorical questions. After the murder of the Governor of Buenos Aires, the Old Woman urges Candide to flee to avoid being burned alive: 'Il n'y avait pas un moment à perdre; mais comment se séparer de Cunégonde, et où se réfugier?' (13:69-71). For the resolution of the dilemma the reader must move on quickly to the next chapter. New possibilities are teasingly signalled at the end of the Eldorado episode as Candide exhorts Cacambo, and the reader, to follow him into the future: 'Marchons vers la Cayenne, embarquons-nous, et nous verrons ensuite quel royaume nous pourrons acheter' (18:175-76). The start of the Old Woman's story in Chapter 11 is precipitated by a deictic *enjambement* from the previous chapter (10:59-60).

Surprise effects openly contradict novelistic conventions of fictive realism and techniques of illusion. Recognition scenes, often absurdly attenuated, offer many good examples. At the end of Chapter 3 a mysterious living corpse appears (4:69-72) whose identity as Pangloss is withheld until the reader has embarked on the next chapter. The rediscovery of Cunégonde in Chapter 7 is a remarkably skilful mixture of surprise effect and intertextual parody: 'Quel moment! quelle surprise! il croit voir mademoiselle Cunégonde; il la voyait en effet, c'était elle-même' (7:34-35). Sentences are frequently booby-trapped, and involve a process of attenuation through enumeration, chiasmus or other cumulative device, only to detonate at the last moment with the insertion of a single word that ignites the text in ways that not only surprise the reader but also encourage critical reflection. The opening sentence of Chapter 3, describing the armies drawn up in battle order (3:2-4), exemplifies Voltaire's use of this technique. Similar effects reversing the reader's expectations are achieved by the use of the word 'héros' in the recruiting scene (2:32-35), to be re-used in an ironic change of contextual key in the account of the unheroic slaughter of defenceless villagers (3:17-21). Similarly, in Portsmouth it is good to kill an admiral from time to time 'pour *encourager* les autres' (23:29-30). The Jesuits in Paraguay have everything and the people nothing: 'c'est le chef-d'œuvre de la raison et de la justice' (14:29-30).

Surprise effects are often achieved through a process of collapse or reversal resulting in a jarring dislocation between words and events, plot developments serving as devices for the deflation of Optimistic pretensions. When Pangloss expounds the view that 'les malheurs particuliers font le bien général; de sorte que, plus il y a de malheurs particuliers et plus tout est bien' (4:94-96), the text directs the reader's attention away from Pangloss towards an abrupt change in the weather that heralds the sinking of the ship (and the syllogism) prior to the earthquake (4:96-98). By the time the reader reaches Chapter 11 to hear the Old Woman's story, the rising-falling pattern has become familiar. When the Old Woman declares, 'je touchais au moment de mon bonheur' (11:25-26), we know that the moment to flinch has arrived, and that her idyllic early life as the daughter of a pope and a princess is about to take a turn for the worse.

Candide's symbolic and referential codes reinforce a fragmentary, chaotic vision of the world, but this is not to say that the tale is *actually* dislocated or casually organised as a loose episodic narrative. Voltaire keeps tight control of narrative design and strategy. Recent explorations of binary patterns of narrative, for example, have shown how Chapters 29 and 30 offer a perfectly contoured mirror-image of Chapter 1 with respect to details of characterisation, setting and sub-textual discourse (*14*, pp.283-92). Individual chapters, and paragraphs within chapters, display a similar symmetry. The 'hospitality' scene in the inn with the recruiters in Chapter 3, followed by induction into the army, is reworked almost as a diptych in Chapter 14 where, after a meal, Candide thinks of offering the Paraguayans the benefit of his skills in 'l'exercice bulgare' (14:36). In Eldorado Candide finds himself in another inn receiving hospitality, but this time the welcome is genuine. The replay of the running-the-gauntlet scene that took place at the hands of the Bulgars is executed this time with musicians rather than *baguette*-wielding soldiers, and ushers Candide into the presence of another, very different king from the one who decided Candide's fate at the end of Chapter 2. Receptions, meals, rituals, sexual encounters recur in *Candide* with a narrative frequency that reinforces through contrastive replay, binary parallelism and other structural links an intricately patterned coherence that offers further evidence of Voltaire's superb narrative craftsmanship (*13*, pp.19-23).

The dynamics of *Candide* work their magic above all through a strikingly original and innovative use of the French language, linked to a subtle orchestration of satirical effect, ironic tone and parodic register. The art of *Candide* has traces of the miraculous about it (*40*), but the miracle is carefully calculated, and facilitated by an extraordinary feat of stylisation and a richness of referential codes. The tale still produces an indelible impression of brilliant improvisation and spontaneity. In each chapter high levels of burlesque effect are achieved with deceptive artlessness by means of an astonishing range of slyly-deployed and well-mixed figurative ingredients and satirical devices: euphemism, deixis, litotes, oxymoron, hyperbole, parataxis, paronomasia, polysemy, disjunction, defamiliar-isation, repetition, chiasmus, antiphrasis, antiphony, alternation and attenuation. Voltaire uses these instruments of narrative subversion with almost surgical precision to imbue the text with a lyrical energy that burns as brightly today as it did in the eighteenth century.

4. The Outward Journey

The Castle

Candide's point of departure, the castle of Baron Thunder-ten-Tronckh, somewhere in Westphalia, shares with Eldorado an otherworldliness, although unlike Eldorado this edifice of dreams is built on the shifting sands of its inhabitants' ignorance, prejudice and foolishness. Candide is the bastard son of the Baron's sister who refused to marry the hero's father because the latter was unable to prove more than 'soixante et onze quartiers' (1:10), that is to say, two thousand years of noble lineage. The hierarchical sequence appropriate to feudal protocol, the first 'system' for the reader to think about (*15*, pp.65-66), is reflected in the order of characters presented in the second paragraph, although protocol has been fractured in the opening paragraph by the precedence given to the bastard/hero.

The Baron, 'un des plus puissants seigneurs de la Westphalie' (1:12-13), is followed by a fat Baroness, 'qui [...] s'attirait par là une très grande considération' (1:20), Cunégonde, 'fraîche, grasse, appétissante' (1:23), the Baron's son, 'en tout digne de son père' (1:24) and the 'oracle', Dr Pangloss. The circle closes, and protocol is belatedly restored, with a second reference to 'le petit Candide', who listens to the words of the oracle, 'avec toute la bonne foi de son âge et de son caractère' (1:25-26). Thus, with the exception of Candide, each is fixed in a pre-determined position, in a chain of authority and status, at the head of which is the 'First Cause' figure of 'Monseigneur'.

This is an enclosed, inward-looking world of appearances, a stasis of collective delusions in which the calculations of pre-established harmony are already being mocked. Voltaire evokes with a few rapid, economical strokes the shoddy *optimum* of circumstances in which the hero has been raised, and upon which his knowledge of the world depends. The castle is a state of mind as well as a location. Empty pretensions embody ironic contradictions, indicating that, far from being the stronghold of power and opulence that the inhabitants believe it to be, the castle is a dilapidated old ruin languishing in a provincial German backwater, its feudal glories in the past, and now reduced to banal impoverishment. What passes for baronial grandeur amounts to a door and a few windows, a carpet, some flea-bitten dogs for a pack of hunting hounds, stable-lads for huntsmen and whippers-in, and the local village priest for a Grand Chaplain (1:12-17). The second paragraph ends with one further piece of information about the inhabitants: they are subservient and credulous, necessary preconditions, not only for the acceptance of the fairy-tale of feudal authority, but for other fairy-tales too.

The ground has now been prepared for the star turn, and ultimate guarantor of the castle's illusions, Dr Pangloss. Pangloss has no physical features, no feelings, no doubts and no human qualities other than foolishness and verbosity. If he cannot easily be visualised, he can be heard, and the semic code is easily read in his case. He is, as his name suggests, just a mouth, and his presence crystallises only in a cascade of flawed syllogisms and philosophy-speak. He teaches the three central components of Optimism: the theory of being ('métaphysico'), the theory of God ('théologo') and the theory of the universe ('cosmolo[nigo]logie'), an *enchaînement* that self-destructs with the intrusion of the pejorative 'nigo' (cf. *nigaud*, *10*, pp.31-32; *32*, pp.142-43). As the spokesman/fall-guy for Optimism, Pangloss is the flesh made word, and then into more words, although he will acquire an increasingly painful physicality as the tale develops. For the moment, however, his entry on stage is that of an ideological automaton, whose mechanical catechism leaves no room for doubt or reflection, and invites no response (1:28-31).

Automata can have their mechanisms jammed by small stones, however. The small stones in this case are the causative conjunctions *car* and *aussi* which are used throughout the tale antiphrasally as disconnectives. Here they are used to decouple a comic sequence of *reductio ad absurdum* statements to offer the first major exposure to laughter of the slippery logic of cause-and-effect theory, and of the terminology of Leibnizio-Wolffian argumentation with its ludicrous disregard, in Voltaire's view, of empirical evidence and its confusion between the causal and the coincidental (1:32-43).

The essence of Pangloss has been prefigured in the setting, and the lampooning of Optimism is embedded inferentially in the text well before Pangloss's first speech in the description of the castle's location, architecture, furnishings and social organisation. After Pangloss's first speech the caricatural mimicry of the language of Optimism continues but is swiftly and incongruously transposed into another context: sex. What was abstract, untrue and bereft of human meaning now moves, again by means of the adroit positioning of the lethal *car*, into a human world of nature and sensation, from which Pangloss too is unable to escape. Candide has listened and believed 'innocemment', and a burlesque reorientation of the terms of philosophical discourse now takes place as Voltaire reframes cause-and-effect providentialism in the context of the lovers' sexual arousal (1:44-51).

The old world of metaphysical sophistry is now comically overlaid with the new world of empirical investigation. Out for a stroll in the castle's 'parc', Cunégonde sees Pangloss in the bushes giving 'une leçon de physique expérimentale' to her mother's chamber-maid, 'petite brune très jolie et très docile' (1:55-56). Like all good experimentalists ('beaucoup de dispositions pour les sciences'), she draws conclusions from the observation of facts. She observes the causes and effects, including Pangloss's 'raison suffisante'. Like her Edenic predecessor, she is fired with the urge to be 'savante', and is convinced that she could well be 'la raison suffisante du jeune Candide, qui pouvait aussi être la sienne' (1:52-62). The physicality of the subsequent encounter between the hero and the heroine, an earthy parody of the standard first kiss scene in conventional novels, fuses with the high language of Optimism to produce an erotically-charged moment of low, debunking farce, the change of tense to past historic again dramatising the disruption caused to the harmony upon which the castle's existence is predicated (*32*, pp.142-45).

The last paragraph of Chapter 1 offers a grand display of satirical and parodic pyrotechnics. In a sharp contrast to the reunification of the lovers at the end of the tale, here they meet in what is initially a world of sentimental innocence, in which a heroine drops her handkerchief for retrieval by a chivalrous suitor, and in which lovers meet with blushing cheeks, dry throats and mutual professions of undying love. This scene, arbitrarily but strategically located 'derrière un paravent', takes place in total silence, words being summarily discarded, along with the conventions of courtly *bienséance*. The truth is laid bare; the lovers are simply enjoying each other sexually, no chivalry, no poetry, no lies, no illusions. As their bodies make contact, Voltaire plays ironically with the word 'innocemment' and the clichés of the *roman sensible*: 'elle lui prit innocemment la main; le jeune homme baisa innocemment la main de la jeune demoiselle [...]' (1:68-71).

Like the Baron's claims to status and wealth, and Pangloss's claims to truth and wisdom, chivalric idealism is brought low by a burlesque change of pace and register that ensures that love is displaced by lust. Innocence 'falls' into eroticism, and ignorance into knowledge: 'leurs bouches se rencontrèrent, leurs yeux s'enflammèrent, leurs genoux tremblèrent, leurs mains s'égarèrent' (1:71-73). The ideal of love is never allowed to offer Candide, or the reader, a pretext for retreat from the need to engage with reality and truth, however unpalatable. The Baron, discovering the lovers *in flagrante*, as barons do, 'et voyant cette cause et cet effet', helps Candide out of the door with a final burlesque flourish, 'à grands coups de pied dans le derrière' (1:75). Candide is obliged to take leave of the best of all possible castles for a world outside in which the precepts of the castle's theoretician will be tested against the truths of a *felt* and *observed* experience, a process of cumulative 'defabulation' (*29*, p.34) that will continue until Chapter 30 in a multiplicity of contexts.

Westphalia

As the doors of the castle of Optimism slam shut behind Candide (and the reader), the weather changes. Winter and a winter of the spirit set in as Candide, driven by cold and hunger, makes for the nearby town and his first encounter with evil. The search for, and consumption of, food plays an important role in *Candide*. Hunger, like sex, fuels the urge to survive (*29*), and keeps the hero and the narrative on the move. The needs of the body drive the disorientated Candide, still yearning for a lost pseudo-Paradise and a lost love (2:2-3), towards the nearest inn, and also towards the arena of the Seven Years' War, 'the most hellish war that was ever fought' (D7931).

In Valdberghoff-trarbk-dickdorff two recruiting sergeants dressed in the notorious blue uniform of Prussian grenadiers, are looking for cannon-fodder. In the false sanctuary of the Westphalian 'cabaret', Candide unknowingly assents to be measured up for conscription in a scene in which the hero and the two recruiters converse on one level, and the authorial voice converses with the reader on another. The recruiters offer not only to pay for Candide's meal, but also give him a few coins for his pocket, an act of cynical deception accompanied by an aphorism from one of the recruiters, ironically inappropriate in the circumstances, but which in fact will prove to have illuminated the *conte,* and in particular the encounter with

Jacques in Chapters 3-4 : 'les hommes ne sont faits que pour se
secourir les uns les autres' (2:20-21). Candide can only agree:
'c'est ce que monsieur Pangloss m'a toujours dit, et je vois bien
que tout est au mieux' (2:22-24).

Blissfully unaware of the implications of taking the King's
shilling, Candide is marched off in chains to experience the
brutalities of military training (2:31-34), not entirely a negative
experience in retrospect as he does emerge toughened up
physically, once he has recovered from his flogging, and with
practical skills that will stand him in good stead. As the heading
to Chapter 2 indicates, a process of becoming has started.
Chapter 2 reflects binary features of composition common to
many other chapters (*13*, pp.7-25). In the first half of the
chapter the general pattern of an encounter with soldiers, an
entrapment, a capture, an interrogation, pain, and resolution in
the context of recruitment (2:9-40) is repeated in the second
half with a more purposeful hero in the context of the urge to
desert and recover his freedom (2:42-45), whereupon approval
is replaced by disapproval (2:47-57). Punishment for desertion
involves running a gauntlet between two ranks of two thousand
men thirty-six times, the sticks used in Candide's training
having now been replaced by the famous Prussian *baguettes*
(ramrods). Candide is flayed from neck to buttocks, and begs
for the *coup de grâce*. The King of the Bulgars sees in Candide,
'[qui] avait déjà un peu de peau' (2:67-68), not a deserter but
'un jeune métaphysicien fort ignorant des choses de ce monde'.
With an eye to favourable press coverage, the monarch agrees
to show mercy, and permits Candide's torn body to be healed,
and we are left with the impression that metaphysics is the real
'crime du patient'. The whole chapter can be seen as a
vulgarised debate on Lockean principles of liberty.

The description of the battle between the Bulgars and the
Abars in Chapter 3 was almost certainly coloured by Voltaire's
memories of the Battle of Rossbach, one of the bloodiest of the
Seven Years' War, and about which he had received graphic
information in November 1757 (D7477; *25*, pp.84-85). The

first two paragraphs present the flamboyant spectacle of the armies drawn up for battle, and provide one of the best examples of Voltaire's ability in *Candide* to promote the destruction of Optimistic theory by means of sharply etched, almost cinematically vivid, tableaux. The hope/expectation curve rises in the second sentence to the evocative sound of a list of pleasure-giving musical instruments, into which Voltaire slips an unexpected sting in the tail (see p.30, above). The images of military splendour and pomp collapse abruptly, and the reader's expectations are deflated when harmony reveals itself to be nothing more than the hellish din of gunfire (3:2-4).

What starts off as a pretty picture of toy soldiers 'renversés' by toy guns quickly fades before the ugly realities of war. Associations with Leibnizio-Wolffism are consolidated with a play on statistics as the cold calculation of a Wolffian good-evil balance sheet offers an Optimistic perspective on the casualties. The terminology of Optimism, used to such comic effect in Chapter 1, is redeployed in more chilling circumstances as the cannon first take out 'environ neuf à dix mille coquins'. The horror of individual suffering is softened by the neutralising effects of mathematical approximation, and empathy is reduced to a minimum. The tension (for the reader) between *what* is being described and *how* it is being described, between events and Optimistic obfuscations of events, increases with an effective use of antiphrasis as the muskets remove from the 'meilleur des mondes' nine to ten thousand 'coquins qui en infectaient la surface' (3:6-7).

Human realities then come into focus as the 'coquins' become 'hommes' in the next sentence, which describes how bayonets were 'la raison suffisante de la mort de quelques milliers d'hommes' (3:7-8). Mutual mass-slaughter has been carried out in a few lines of laconic prose from which all sense of compassion and horror has been excised on the surface of the narrative, but which, by a characteristically Voltairean trick of ironic displacement, has been intensified at the sub-textual level. Pangloss is not present, but his voice can be clearly heard, and through Candide's 'innocent eye' the consequences of his teachings clarify, at least for the reader. The hero is still 'un jeune métaphysicien', and while the warring armies listen to God's blessing on their respective causes, he can only turn his eyes away from the carnage and meditate on causes and effects (3:13-14).

Candide's walk through the war-zone is the walk of a philosopher. As he picks his way around the spilled brains and amputated limbs, the false consolations of Optimism accompany him, and blind him to the evidence of his own eyes. All is still for the best. The casualty list itemises the human cost of war, but the terrible mathematics of totalism, the Wolffian calculation, continue to deny the true significance of Pope's 'partial evils'. The finality of death is masked by the Christian-providentialist promise of salvation as the 'coquins' become 'âmes' (3:8-9). The village has been destroyed, but 'selon les lois du droit public'. Girls have been raped and eviscerated, but have satisfied the natural needs of 'quelques héros' (3:17-20). 'Le tout' means nothing if not a balanced compromise. The Leibnizian principle of compensation in creation is technically intact, though morally bankrupt. War was for Voltaire one of the greatest of all evils, but its lessons are lost on Candide, who dreams only of Cunégonde.

Holland

Voltaire's attack on organised religion in his *contes* was unremitting. *Candide* is littered with hostile allusions to theological matters, and features a wide range of religious figures, usually operating in contexts of sexual deviation, greed, dishonesty, lust, rape or murder. There are also a number of parodic scriptural references and echoes: an edenic hero and heroine enjoying the fruits of knowledge, the sheep/lost sheep of Eldorado, the cultivation of the garden/Lord's vineyard, Candide's/Christ's entry into the holy city of Surinam/Jerusalem, Candide's/Abraham's subterfuge of passing Cunégonde/Sarah off as his sister, and the parable of the Good Samaritan, shadowed in the portrayal of Jacques (*19*, pp.124-31).

Chapters 3-4 encompass an exchange with a Dutch Calvinist preacher and his wife, the first encounter with Jacques and, towards the end of Chapter 3, the sudden reappearance of a grotesquely damaged Pangloss. After leaving the 'membres palpitants' of the Bulgar village behind, Candide's hopes rise as he arrives in Holland. He has heard that the country is rich and pious, and therefore probably tolerant and charitable. This hopeful assumption is abruptly dashed as the sober Dutch Christians, from whom Candide begs for help on the streets of Amsterdam, threaten him with imprisonment 'pour lui apprendre à vivre' (3:35-38). He tries his luck with a preacher who, promisingly, has just delivered a long sermon on charity, but the preacher's interrogation of Candide hints darkly at a fanatical intolerance: 'Que venez-vous faire ici? y êtes-vous pour la bonne cause?' (3:41-42).

The question, deceptively couched in Optimistic terminology, triggers a mechanical Panglossian response, in a knock-about exchange of comic misunderstanding, reminiscent in technique of the recruiting scene in Chapter 2. Candide unreels an *enchaînement* of causes and effects, again reflecting the persistent legacy of Pangloss (3:42-48). The preacher addresses Candide in a Quaker-like manner as 'Mon ami', but Quaker-like charity does not materialise, as Candide heads off a menacing abstract question about the Pope with a plea for food. He is pronounced a 'coquin', and sent on his way covered in the contents of a chamberpot emptied over him by the preacher's coarse wife, a burlesque ending to a scene in which religious intolerance merges with the sewage tipped over the starving hero's head: 'Ô Ciel! à quel excès se porte le zèle de la religion chez les dames!' (3:55-56).

In the next, sharply contrasting, scene Candide discovers to his surprise that his expectations of charity and compassion will be met by a heretic, 'un bon anabaptiste, nommé Jacques'

(3:57-58). Jacques's presence in the tale is fleeting, but his contribution to Candide's moral apprenticeship colours indelibly the tale's ideological landscape. Since leaving the Baron's castle, Candide has passed through rejection and loneliness, cold and hunger, torture and intolerance. His body has known pain, and he has been witness to the pain of others. He has learned that evil exists and, as a Lockean hero in the making, he has *felt* its presence, but has preferred so far to take refuge from the lessons of experience in the teachings of Pangloss.

Jacques is an Anabaptist, a member of an unauthorised sect with its origins in the Reformation, professing the baptism of adults. Voltaire had praised the virtues of the Anabaptists in the *Essai sur les mœurs*: a minimum of dogma (and therefore dispute), deistic, unitarian tendencies, and an emphasis on practical, socially-directed benevolence. Jacques is the counter-example of humanity in what is otherwise a world of executioners and executed. His portrait coincides quite closely with that of the attractively quirky Quaker in the first letter of the *Lettres philosophiques* (1734), moral qualities and a tendency to silence on philosophical matters predominating in both. To Jacques, Candide's suffering is not a 'partial evil' to be weighed against a greater good, but an absolute evil to be confronted. Beneath the disgusting, excrement-covered figure in front of him, he recognises a common humanity, 'un de ses frères, un être à deux pieds sans plumes, qui avait une âme' (3:59-60). For Jacques Candide is not the object to which all victims are reduced before being slaughtered in good conscience, like the 'coquins' of the battlefield, or the raped and dismembered villagers to whose plight Candide himself had been so shockingly indifferent.

Jacques works to earn a living as a textile-manufacturer in the unphilosophical world of commerce and international trade. The first example in the tale of linkage between happiness and work, he contributes to the general prosperity of society, and is an ideal model of civic duty whose life is driven by virtue not greed (*25*, pp.65-66). A pragmatist and the embodiment of enlightened self-interest (*24*, p.69), he provides Candide with sanctuary, and in offering the hero work (3:60-63), hints at a way forward to be advocated later on by a wiser Candide, but seen here erroneously only as a long-awaited confirmation that all is for the best (3:65).

Candide is still Pangloss's creature, but Jacques's example will lead to changes. Under the Anabaptist's influence philosophy releases its grip slightly, and the ability to be moved to compassion, and to take action to relieve suffering, becomes a possibility for the first time. The first beneficiary of this change in Candide will be an unnamed 'gueux', whose sudden appearance provides further eloquent testimony to what can happen to the human body in the best of all possible worlds (3:69-72). This time Candide does not avert his gaze from the grotesque, almost carnivalesque (*22*, p.85) spectacle. He is 'plus ému encore de compassion que d'horreur' (4:1), and immediately dispenses charity with the two florins given to him by Jacques. After learning that the 'fantôme' is actually Pangloss, and seeing that the latter is suffering too much to answer questions, he offers him shelter and food in Jacques's stable (4:5-13). The earlier charity-denying scene with the Dutch preacher is now reworked with Candide providing the model response to human suffering in the light of Jacques's example.

Pangloss brings news of the fate of 'le plus beau des châteaux' and that 'chef-d'œuvre de la nature', Cunégonde. Upon learning of the latter's death, Candide faints with shock, but in contrast to the care he has lavished upon Pangloss, the latter can only revive Candide with 'un peu de mauvais vinaigre', originally in the La Vallière manuscript version 'urine de vache' – possibly an echo of the chamberpot scene (*13*, pp.32-33). Candide voices dangerous doubts about providence when Pangloss informs him that Cunégonde, disembowelled and raped 'autant qu'on peut l'être', is dead (4:17-18).

Pangloss's account of the annihilation of the castle is followed by his first extended philosophical exchange with Candide, if the nose-spectacle speech in Chapter 1, during which Candide had been just a passive and credulous listener, is excluded. Pangloss explains his own brush with evil arising from the 'leçon de physique expérimentale' given to the chambermaid (1:54-58), now named as Paquette. Candide cross-examines Pangloss closely for the first time on causes and effects, and on the *raison suffisante* for his mentor's syphilitic condition. 'Hélas! dit l'autre, c'est l'amour: l'amour, le consolateur du genre humain, le conservateur de l'univers, l'âme de tous les êtres sensibles, le tendre amour' (4:33-35). The rhetoric of sensibility adopted by Pangloss in his answer is sustained in Candide's response for half a sentence before being punctured by the usual burlesque collapse in the second half with a matching sentimental declamation: 'Hélas, dit Candide, je l'ai connu, cet amour, ce souverain des cœurs, cette âme de notre âme; il ne m'a jamais valu qu'un baiser et vingt coups de pied au cul' (4:36-38).

The illusion of love, like that of philosophical systems, shatters once again on the hard Lockean rock of sense-based experience as Pangloss describes his contraction of syphilis at the very moment of savouring 'les délices du paradis'. The stark fact of syphilitic infection negates the poetry of love, and its burlesque debasement is prolonged by another *enchaînement* in which Pangloss traces a convoluted genealogy of venereal disease, reminiscent in its misplaced claims to dignity of Candide's own troublesome 'arbre généalogique' (1:10). The overt intention is to demonstrate once more that all is for the best (4:55-59). The covert intention is to show how the 'arbre généalogique' demonstrates the inexorable dominion of evil through space and time, and this would have been a particularly effective paragraph for readers in a pre-antibiotics age. Pangloss's statement contains two errors, to be added to the erroneous reporting of Cunégonde's death, namely that Paquette had died and that he himself was dying. The errorcount associable with Optimism, as well as the body-count, is rising.

The perverse currents of Optimistic argument swirl around as Panglossian logic twists back on itself. Pangloss notes that so far syphilis is endemic only to Europe, 'comme la controverse', but what should be a consolation turns for the reader into the prospect of further despair as Pangloss insists that while other nations might not yet have syphilis, their turn will come (4:64-65). Meanwhile, syphilis has made 'un merveilleux progrès parmi nous', especially among soldiers. When thirty thousand troops (the numbers have escalated since Chapter 3) face another thirty thousand in battle order, Pangloss observes cheerfully that there will be about twenty thousand on each side with the pox (4:65-70). The human cost of such Optimistic 'success' is diminished by the substitution of the word 'stipendaires' (i.e. mercenaries) for 'hommes' (4:66) which, like 'coquins' in Chapter 2, conveys a *tout est au mieux* inference obscuring evil realities.

Candide prefers action to words: 'Voilà qui est admirable [. . .] mais il faut vous faire guérir' (4:71-72). The philosopher, 'les yeux morts' (3:70), can resolve the metaphysical problem of his own suffering in the 'meilleur des mondes' with Optimistic palliatives, but is unable to resolve the practical problem of his own survival. The lethal irrelevance and futility of system-building, with its action-denying consequences, has been brilliantly illustrated with caricatural simplicity and bite. Jacques, a modern version of the Good Samaritan (Luke, 10: 30-36) responds immediately to Candide's request for help, and Candide's experience of the world benefits positively for the second time by an example of human solidarity and *bienfaisance*. 'Le bonhomme' *feels* in ways denied to system-builders. Touched by Candide's pleas, Jacques offers Pangloss his protection, and pays for a cure (4:78-79). Evil makes another small, but significant, concession to human action. The cure costs Pangloss an eye and an ear, appropriately symbolic disfigurements for a philosopher impervious to the evidence of his senses. The Optimist cannot see or hear properly, but Jacques can still find useful work for him to do, and puts his skills to good use as an accountant. As a good Wolffian, Pangloss can do sums (4:80-82).

Before the Dutch scenes come to an end an important exchange takes place between Pangloss and Jacques that goes to the heart of the Optimistic debate. After two months of tranquillity, Jacques's international business interests call him to Lisbon, and he sets sail with his 'deux philosophes'. For Pangloss, life with Jacques has merely confirmed that 'tout était on ne peut mieux' (4:85-86). Jacques disagrees, and questions the deterministic implications. The human condition is dynamic, not static, as his own actions have demonstrated with resulting beneficial effects on the quality of life now enjoyed by Pangloss and Candide. The order of nature is susceptible to human will and action, and Jacques's characterisation embodies a view of good and evil arising, not as part of a given order of creation, but as a consequence, at least in part, of human intervention. Echoing Hobbes and taking a phrase from Plautus, Jacques tells his guests that men were not born wolves but have become wolves through their own actions and decisions, and as a result of their free will.

The self-referential circles of the text close again as the war between the Abars and Bulgars is recalled, but this time stripped of the lying gloss of Optimistic jargon. The conjunction *et* introduces sequential, not consequential, action and replaces the ironically disjunctive *car* of the earlier scene: God did not give man cannon capable of firing twenty-four-pounders, or bayonets: 'et ils se sont fait des baïonnettes et des canons pour se détruire' (4:86-90). Pangloss, 'le docteur borgne', can only respond with his famous self-destroying axiom, built around another ironic antiphrasis (4:93-96). As usual, events in the real world cut short philosophical speculation, and the argument between Pangloss and Jacques closes with a darkening of clouds and the onset of violent storms as Jacques's ship approaches Lisbon.

Portugal

Candide completes his moral apprenticeship with Jacques against the backdrop of the great earthquake, and the last scene with the Anabaptist takes place on board the ship chartered for the business trip to Lisbon. Scenes on board ships in *Candide* are always interesting interludes. There are four altogether, one of which extends over two chapters (11-12). The image of a ship at sea (7, p.28), steered by a captain and crew who know little of the mice in the hold, who in turn have no conception of the ship's design or purpose, was used by Voltaire in a letter to Frederick the Great in 1736 (D1139) to represent a deistic view of the human condition. In *Candide* the ship of deism sinks, the relevance of abstract systems again fading before urgent issues of life and death.

As the ship breaks up, half of the passengers die in 'angoisses inconcevables', while the other half can only scream and pray helplessly (5:1-5). Chaos triumphs, but the struggle for meaningful ways in which to challenge the chaos continues with Jacques '[qui] aidait un peu à la manœuvre', and who has maximised his chances of survival by getting to the top deck (5:1-8). His efforts are frustrated by 'un matelot furieux' who knocks him out but who, losing his balance as a result of this act of gratuitous malice, is himself tossed overboard and entangled in broken rigging (5:8-12). Candide and Pangloss now witness the injured 'bon Jacques' perform his last act of human solidarity and self-sacrificing *bienfaisance*. He rescues the undeserving sailor, but in so doing falls into the raging seas, and drowns under the latter's unpitying gaze. Action and inaction, self-sacrifice and callous indifference, enlightened self-interest and individual selfishness are dramatically juxtaposed. Candide, however, no longer plays the dummy's role in a ventriloquist's act, and in this scene Pangloss is the only character tagged with the damning designation, 'philosopher' (5:18).

The seeds of Jacques's values have been planted, and soon produce fragile shoots. Candide sees Jacques surface momentarily, and tries to dive in to save him. The paralysis that held him in check among the wounded in the Abar-Bulgar battle zone has gone, but his rediscovered sense of shared humanity and his reawakened instinct to take action can still be frustrated by Pangloss, from whom ideological independence has not yet been completely achieved: 'Il veut se jeter après lui dans la mer: le philosophe Pangloss l'en empêche, en lui prouvant que la rade de Lisbonne avait été formée exprès pour que cet anabaptiste s'y noyât' (5:15-20). Optimistic 'proofs' are again undermined by events as the ship founders and all the passengers perish, with the arbitrary exceptions of Candide, Pangloss and 'ce brutal de matelot qui avait noyé le vertueux anabaptiste' (5:22). The dramatic qualities of the narrative are striking. There is little literary ornamentation, but instead a tightly focused concentration on events and facts, an acceleration of pace and a sense of actuality accentuated by the skilful alternation of the present, imperfect and past historic tenses.

The earthquake starts immediately upon their arrival in the city, and narrative pace again quickens as Voltaire injects another of those carefully calculated, jarring notes of realism that achieve their shock-effects at an intensely visual level. The statistics of evil and death rise again as thirty thousand crushed citizens of Lisbon join the thirty thousand battlefield casualties and the forty thousand victims of syphilis. The language of destruction and confusion predominates throughout, reproducing the effects of the tremors at a textual level (5:28-49). The earthquake in *Candide* is nothing less than a visualisation, not just of a natural disaster, but of the violent incoherence of the human condition in general, 'this lasting hurricane of horror' (D7931).

Three reactions to the devastation are registered, the first two of which have Optimistic connotations: the sailor relishes the opportunity to loot the dead and injured, Pangloss asks what the 'raison suffisante' for the catastrophe might be, and the third reaction, human, engaged, fearful, and above all untainted by the distancing effects of Optimism, is Candide's (5:38). The sailor picks the pockets of the dead, and as he buys the favours of a passing prostitute Pangloss reproaches him for contravening the laws of universal reason, only to be met with a curse and a contemptuous replay of his own words (5:48-49).

Despite the setbacks, Panglossian cause-and-effect ratiocination continues undeterred by its own irrelevance. Candide, injured by falling stones, and addressing Pangloss in the familiar 'tu' form, asks for oil and wine for his wounds in another scene with echoes of the parable of the Good Samaritan. Unlike Jacques, however, Pangloss offers only disputatious argument. He is more alarmed by Candide's demotion of causalism from a certainty to a probability than by Candide's injuries (5:53-61). In the end, both are rescued from their plight by the actions of others, and the light of Jacques's example shines out once more as Candide *and Pangloss* join in the collective rescue operation to save survivors. Human solidarity and enlightened self-interest bring rewards, and they are given 'un aussi bon dîner qu'on le pouvait dans un tel désastre' (5:66-67). Optimism soon resurfaces, however, when Pangloss consoles the grieving citizens of Lisbon with an *enchaînement* of providentialist propositions assuring them that the fate of the city was pre-ordained, and that events could not have turned out differently (5:68-73). Unwisely he engages in further debate on the subject of evil and sin in another entrapment scene masterminded by a man dressed in the black garb of an agent of the Inquisition. The suffering body is about to teach Candide and his mentor another painful lesson about the dangers of metaphysical speculation.

The second half of Chapter 5 and the whole of Chapter 6 bristle with satirical barbs aimed at superstition, intolerance, heresy, ritual, academic dogmatism, human credulity and the taste for blood. The principal target is the Inquisition, about which Voltaire had gathered much information from Dellon's

1688 *Relation sur l'Inquisition de Goa* (*19*, p.128). With three quarters of the Lisbon population destroyed, the Inquisitors, 'les sages du pays', decide to accept the view of the University of Coimbra that the ceremonial roasting of a few people will serve as an infallible prophylactic against further earthquakes. The compact tableau, emptying church ritual of any sense of spirituality in its depiction of the burning of the two Jews and the Biscayen (see also Cunégonde's angle on the scene offered in Chapter 8), is a good example of the way in which Voltaire mixes farce and realism with a deceptively inconsequential style of narration that serves only to darken the horror. History records the fact that no less than three *auto-da-fés* occurred in Lisbon between 1756 and 1758 (*7*, p.138). Here, as elsewhere, Voltaire's use of facts, like his use of events and people drawn from contemporary life, are dynamic features of the narrative and have an ideological function. They blend unnervingly with the fictive qualities of the *conte* format as a man from Bilbao, guilty of infringing consanguinity laws, and two Portuguese Jews who refused to eat pork (a much-prized dish in the Baron's castle), are seized, along with Pangloss, punished for reported heresies, and Candide, for having listened 'avec un air d'approbation' (6:10-13).

Candide, by now less philosophically burdened than Pangloss, has his death-sentence commuted, but is ceremonially lashed 'en cadence, pendant qu'on chantait'. The others are burned, except for Pangloss who, inexplicably, is hanged. The ground shakes again with renewed violence, nature remaining unimpressed by a spectacle designed for the benefit of the superstitious to placate it (6:22-25). The purpose of the earthquake in *Candide*, unlike its purpose in the *Poème sur le désastre de Lisbonne*, is not just to remind the reader that there is a question mark over God's benevolence. Here the emphasis is on the absurdity and futility of attempts to account dogmatically for the mysteries of the human condition, whether those attempts are manifested in public burnings or in the equally grotesque 'raisonnements' of metaphysicians (*29*, pp.113-15). The scene is also part of a sequence attacking collusion between Church and State, a point about the trial that is clarified in Chapters 8-9, linking the *auto-da-fé* to the arming of the Moroccans in Chapter 12, and to the enslavement of negroes in Chapter 19. Optimism hangs from the gallows of the Inquisition, and Candide has now reached a critical stage in the testing of the cruel philosophy: 'Si c'est ici le meilleur des mondes possibles, que sont donc les autres? [...] Ô mon cher anabaptiste! le meilleur des hommes, faut-il que vous ayez été noyé dans le port! Ô mademoiselle Cunégonde! la perle des filles, faut-il qu'on vous ait fendu le ventre!' (6:28-35).

The last question is addressed promptly when the Old Woman leads Candide away from the flames of the *auto-da-fé,* soothes his injuries, and takes him through the backstreets of Lisbon to a house where the resurrected Cunégonde is waiting. A farcical recognition scene between hero and heroine is then enacted, a delicious parody of the story of the lovers in Prévost's sentimental novel *Manon Lescaut* (7:30-54; *8,* pp.xxvi-xxxviii). In this brilliant example of satirical intertextuality the intense sensibility of the famous Des Grieux-Manon reunion is replaced by an anti-sentimental, burlesque knock-about during which Cunégonde summarily shrugs off the tale of rape and disembowelment recounted earlier by Pangloss: 'Si fait [...] mais on ne meurt pas toujours de ces deux accidents' (7:45-47). Cunégonde has survived to tell of her rescue from the ruined castle by a Bulgar Captain and her acquisition in Holland by the Jewish merchant Don Issacar. The real reason for the *auto-da-fé* now emerges. The Grand Inquisitor has used the burning to intimidate Don Issacar into agreeing to an arrangement whereby he can share the favours of Cunégonde who thus was able to watch the burnings, the hanging of Pangloss and the flogging of Candide at close quarters from a privileged seat with other ladies of the town as if it were a night out at the theatre (8:51-55).

Events now unfold rapidly as Cunégonde's owners arrive
to enjoy her favours, only to be greeted by 'notre bon
Westphalien', who puts his Bulgar training to good effect and
runs them both through with his sword. Again the parodic
intertextual note is sustained as Candide follows in the steps of
Prévost's Des Grieux to become a murderer, a stranger to
himself, driven to violence by passion: 'quand on est amoureux,
jaloux et fouetté par l'Inquisition, on ne se connaît plus' (9:34-
35). The Old Woman, ever resourceful and practical, facilitates
their escape to the New World. There the Governor of Buenos
Aires determines to have Cunégonde for himself, and the
heroine is reconciled to her fate after listening to advice on
survival tactics from the Old Woman, who also advises Candide
to flee to avoid arrest from the Cadiz police who have been
pursuing him across the Atlantic. Again pragmatism triumphs
over sentiment as Candide takes the Old Woman's advice
(13:64-69), and reluctantly leaves Cunégonde, unknowingly
abandoning her to the charms of Don Fernando. The New
World seems to be very much like the Old, with the hero
caught between the shadows of the past, the dangers of the
present, and the uncertainties of the future.

5. The Gold Standard: Eldorado

Drawing on well-established conventions of utopic writing, Voltaire's Eldorado presents a sequence of tableaux in which familiar ideas on economics, government and religion, typical of the mid-eighteenth-century Enlightenment, are brought into rather hazy focus. There is no detailed exploration of any single issue, and Voltaire took care to invest the episode with an ambiance of remoteness and isolation. His purpose could have been primarily satirical (17). The importance of the land of gold in *Candide* lies less in its specific details than in its general symbolism as a location of idealism through which Candide must travel before he can re-engage purposefully with the world as it is. Eldorado is always in the future – not an *optimum,* but in its general outlines a progressivist vision of a better world that challenges the Optimists' claim that perfection is already in place. Eldorado has nothing of the fixity of the Baron's castle about it, but is rather in a process of becoming as the emphasis on dynamic activity suggests. Moreover, Voltaire's picture of Eldoradan life is not entirely free of ambiguities and reservations (16, p.142).

In the scenes in Paraguay, Candide is accompanied by Cacambo, a Figaro-like valet whom he acquired in Cadiz (8, p.xviii). Cacambo is a South American quadroon by birth with an impressive list of careers behind him as 'enfant de chœur, sacristain, matelot, moine, facteur, soldat, laquais' (14:3-4). He joins Jacques and the Old Woman as one of the three main positive forces in the *conte,* and like the Old Woman, but unlike Jacques, he is a survivor. He takes the initiative, and facilitates Candide's transition from the world of abstractions, illusions and nostalgia to the world of action and reality. After the

strange encounter with the Oreillons in Chapter 16, in which
the Rousseauist thesis about the natural goodness of man had
been tested and found wanting, Candide and Cacambo arrive,
thanks to Cacambo's resourcefulness, at the borders of
Eldorado. The pace of the narrative decelerates sharply in
Chapters 17 and 18, and the effect is to generate a mood of
reflective calm. These two chapters are further distanced from
the rest of the text by a style of writing in which the usual
mischievous edge and linguistic *brio* are noticeably subdued.
Nevertheless, the Eldoradan episode is not a totally self-
contained interlude. This is not just a snap-shot of Voltaire's
ideal state, unrelated either to what precedes it or to what
happens next. Eldorado interlocks with the rest of the tale, and
has a particularly close bearing on interpretations of the tale's
conclusion.

After their narrow escape from the *mise en broche* at the
hands of the Oreillons, Candide and Cacambo are temporarily
disorientated and dispirited, the world seemingly offering them
only a choice between degrees of unpleasantness (17:1-9). The
path to Eldorado is not easily negotiated, but while the
landscape is wild and dangerous, its hostility to hopeful and
determined travellers is not an insuperable obstacle to progress.
For the first time in *Candide* nature is benevolent. Wild fruits
sustain them, and after a month they end up on the banks of an
unknown river lined with coconut-trees 'qui soutinrent leur vie
et leurs espérances' (17:16-20), luck and their own
resourcefulness having helped them on their way. The account
of their arrival is charged with symbolism, though entirely free
from any hint of the fabulous, the miraculous or the fantastic
that contemporary readers might have expected. At the same
time, parodic echoes of journeys to fabulous places in the
medieval *roman d'aventures* can be easily detected – the journey
to Torelore in *Aucassin et Nicolette*, itself a parody, springs most
readily to mind here. The description of Eldorado itself is not
entirely a figment of Voltaire's imagination (6, p.103), but it
has an overlay of symbolic features that crystallise more clearly

when compared to other parts of the text, especially Chapter 1 and Chapter 30.

Unlike the 'parc' in the Baron's castle, and unlike Pococuranté's garden, 'le pays était cultivé pour le plaisir comme pour le besoin: partout l'utile était agréable' (17:38-39). Handsome men and beautiful women ride in splendid carriages drawn by 'moutons rouges' (llamas?), capable of outpacing the fastest horse. Eldorado is a place of spaciousness and 'filtered luminosity' (*16*, p.150) radiating benevolence, beneficence and harmony. The light of Eldorado casts an ironic shadow over Candide and Cacambo, who can only observe the scene with uncomprehending European eyes, and evaluate it in the light of unworthy European values. One thing does become clear to Candide, however. The Panglossian assumption of an *optimum* in Westphalia is now definitely vulnerable: 'Voilà pourtant [...] un pays qui vaut mieux que la Westphalie' (17:46-47).

The discovery of Eldorado comes at the point where both the old and the new worlds have been found wanting (17:4-10). Following conventions of utopic fiction, Eldorado offers a polarised mirror-image of the values and attitudes of outside 'normality'. Iconic symbols of wealth – precious metals and stones – have no value here beyond the utilitarian. This Eldorado is not a metal-based economy in spite of its name, its wealth being based on what is produced, an echo perhaps of Voltaire's physiocratic sympathies that will be heard again at the end of the tale. Children, dressed in gold- and silver-emblazoned clothes, play marbles with priceless jewels. They are not the royal princes that European logic assumes them to be, but merely 'petits gueux' (17:60). Their indifference to the 'value' of their toys is matched only by the greed of the travellers in wishing to pocket them. The opening scene invites the reader to reconsider the relationship of wealth to happiness.

Another inn scene then takes place, its pleasures contrasting sharply with the dangers, deceits and disasters encountered in other inns. Here there are no predators,

philosophers or vagabonds, only honest people doing useful
work: 'pour la plupart des marchands et des voituriers' (17:92-
93). Unlike the meal offered to Candide by the Bulgar
recruiters, with which this scene has a carefully configured
binary relationship (*13*, pp.21-23), the acceptance of food does
not spring a trap. Attempts by the travellers to pay for the meal
with the diamonds just picked up in the street results only in
laughter and the explanation that meals are subsidised in
Eldoradan inns in the interests of trade, one of the few
references to a specific example of an Eldoradan government
policy. Trade and the values of a merchant class, already
exemplified by Jacques, are clearly intended as key features of
Eldoradan life, although how mercantilism operates in practical
terms, and to what purpose in a country without currency or
profit motive, is not explored.

The social and economic disorientation of Candide and
Cacambo is accentuated by a pointedly unwarranted apology
from the innkeeper for the frugality of the meal, and the
paradoxical assurance that the travellers will find a higher
quality of service elsewhere in Eldorado. Again they reflect on
where they could be, Candide noting that it was almost
certainly the place where all really was well: 'Et, quoi qu'en dît
maître Pangloss, je me suis souvent aperçu que tout allait mal
en Westphalie' (17:114-17). Enlightenment comes from a wise
'vieillard', one of the standard tropes in Voltairean fiction. The
conventional master-servant relationship between Candide and
Cacambo now changes temporarily to one based on talent
rather than class. Elsewhere in the tale Candide seems to have
no linguistic difficulties (*7*, p.195), but with the exception of
Spanish, the New World languages of the Oreillons and the
Eldoradans defeat him. Cacambo knows how to speak
Peruvian, the language of Eldorado, and this unexplained
linguistic advantage (and why should it be explained in a *conte*?)
enables him to seize the initiative in the conversation with the
Old Man. In due course, the Candide-Cacambo relationship
will consolidate an important *leitmotif* in the later stages of the

tale relating to friendship, and the value of shared human feelings and experience (*24*, p.33).

In Chapter 18 the Old Man tells of the origins of Eldorado in the 'étonnantes révolutions du Pérou', and in an account that bears a passing resemblance to Montesquieu's story of the Troglodytes in Letters 11-14 of the *Lettres persanes,* the travellers learn that Eldorado is a kingdom which the Incas abandoned in order to pursue foreign conquests, an unwise policy resulting in their slaughter at the hands of the Spanish. Learning the lesson of this experience, the Eldoradans have severed their links with the world to secure their survival. They have turned their backs on evil, but in contrast to the Thunder-ten-Tronckh situation, they are quite aware of evil's presence in the world, and of their vulnerability to it. The policy of withdrawal behind closed frontiers imposes constraints on freedom that mysteriously carry with them the consent of the people, 'et c'est ce qui nous a conservé notre innocence et notre félicité' (18:23-27). This policy, together with the natural protection afforded by the surrounding terrain, gives Eldorado the air of a mental and physical fortress existing in self-imposed isolation from the mainstream of human affairs, neither importing nor exporting goods, people or ideas.

The travellers are particularly curious about religion, always for Voltaire the litmus test of a society's health. Candide and Cacambo assume wrongly that there is no religion in Eldorado, and the Old Man's response allows the issue of sectarian strife to be raised obliquely (18:43-45). Cacambo presses the Old Man for further details with what the latter can only regard as 'questions singulières' that only 'les gens de votre monde' could pose. Most of the information about this aspect of Eldoradan civil life reflects Voltaire's views on the merits of the deistic ethic, and contains few surprises except perhaps for the baffling reference to worship of the deity as being a nocturnal activity (18:45). There are no sects, no dogma, no professional clergy, no superstition, no intolerance, no *auto-da-fés*, and above all no religious meddling in political matters.

Nothing is asked of the deity, prayers consisting only of giving thanks for blessings received. Most important of all, the infectious 'rage' of fanaticism has not touched Eldorado (18:62). Approval for all this is signalled to the reader with the promotion of the Old Man to 'bon vieillard' and eventually to 'bon et respectable sage'.

The organisation and administration of civil affairs are not elaborated in any great detail, although a long conversation is reported to have taken place on 'la forme du gouvernement, sur les mœurs, sur les femmes, sur les spectacles publics, sur les arts' (18:35-38). The King of Eldorado is a *roi-philosophe,* whose portrait constrasts sharply with that of the King of the Bulgars (*13*, pp.23-26). In the scene describing the court reception for Candide the royal guards turn out to be pretty girls who receive the strangers in extravagantly sumptuous style: 'les conduisirent aux bains, les vêtirent de robes d'un tissu de duvet de colibri' (18:85-86). The King of Eldorado confounds Candide further when it becomes clear that the abasement of commoners before royalty is not practised, and that it is not necessary in Eldorado to crawl on one's knees or lick the ground in the presence of kings. There is no trace of the cold remoteness of the faceless Bulgar autocrat in this king who greets his guests as equals. Nor will this king form part of the ragged chorus-line of failed monarchs that Candide will meet in Venice in Chapter 26.

Much of the discursive undertow of the Eldoradan episode concerns power relations and the attitude that should be taken towards superior beings, whether gods or kings (*13*, pp.27-28). In Eldorado authority figures are respected, not for the fear that they instil, but for the feelings of natural affection that their beneficence inspires. Beyond that the nature of the King of Eldorado's authority, and the extent of his power over his subjects, remain a matter for speculation. The text simply signals that the king is an enlightened monarch governing by popular consent, and that monarchical rule in Eldorado is a uniting force for social harmony and cohesion. Despite the egalitarian ethos, however, the social structure is still clearly pyramidic. Power is not exercised in an overtly autocratic manner, but covertly the authority of the few governs the lives of the rest, albeit benevolently. The discreet nature of kingly power resurfaces when the two travellers wish to leave Eldorado.

In their tour of the city, Candide and Cacambo learn that there are no courts of justice, no *parlement* or other legislative buildings, and no prisons. Law and order simply exist. Citizens of Eldorado do not commit crimes, or go to war, or display selfish, socially harmful behaviour. Human nature in Eldorado has been purged of wickedness. How this has been achieved is not clear, although Voltaire raises by implication Rousseau's link between the transformation of society and the regeneration of the individual. The civilising effects of art and culture possibly have a role to play here too. Certainly the arts and the sciences are in a healthier state than they prove to be in Paris and Venice.

The vigorous, uncensored pursuit of knowledge can be inferred from the existence of a 'palais des sciences' with its exhibition of scientific instruments (18:108). Science in Eldorado compares favourably with the frivolities that pass for scientific research at the Bordeaux Academy, and seems to have something of the hard-nosed practicality of the science of Diderot's *Encyclopédie* about it. Eldoradan scientists share and communicate the civilising benefits of their knowledge, a far cry from the arcane pursuits of their counterparts in Europe. Music and architecture combine harmoniously to produce beauty and pleasure. There is no reference to literature or the other arts, and metaphysics and philosophy are naturally ignored. As with the countryside surrounding the city-state, the social landscape is also cultivated with a view to making 'l'utile partout agréable'.

From the standpoint of characterisation, the Eldoradans come to life only as part of a homogeneous collectivity. Their group portrait is that of a communal self, and lacks the strong

colours and raw vitality of other crowds in *Candide*. While the
Eldoradans have no problem with boredom, *ennui* might well
be a danger for the two travellers, should they choose to stay.
The word *bonheur* is never mentioned, but the Eldoradans seem
to be happy, or at least they perceive themselves to be happy,
which is perhaps all that matters. The question of self-
perception, and its relationship to self-determination, will arise
again in Chapter 30. Eldorado is the gold standard by which to
measure the inadequacies of the present and the possibilities for
the future. It points backwards to Westphalia and forwards to
Candide's garden in Turkey, a crucially important staging post
in the hero's journey, but not his destination.

As the episode draws to a close, and its possible purpose
as a symbol of human aspiration has been served, narrative
imperatives take over. Candide must move on. He and
Cacambo are representatives of unregenerated humanity, and
after a month Candide finds that the delights of the city of gold
start to pall, reminding us that the values of *Candide* are not
always Candide's (*24*, p.45; *29*, pp.120-21). Assimilation into
the Eldoradan communal self holds few attractions for
Candide, to his discredit perhaps. However, his reservation
raises intriguing question marks: 'Si nous restons ici, nous n'y
serons que comme les autres' (18:123-24).

Ambiguities aside, the Eldoradan experience has been on
the whole educative and beneficial, and Candide returns to his
quest strengthened and more resolute than before. The
prospect of reunion with Cunégonde is no longer a vague
dream but a practical proposition for which Eldorado has
opened up new possibilities, not the least of which are those
that result from the possession of Eldoradan 'fange'. Cacambo
is persuaded (not ordered) to leave with him, and with their
joint decision to return to Europe, 'les deux heureux résolurent
de ne plus l'être' (18:132). In the end, Eldorado has offered
them pleasure but not true happiness, sanctuary but not
purpose. The King wishes them to stay, but understands their
desire to leave. He does not impose his will, but offers them

wise advice instead: 'Vous faites une sottise [...] je sais bien que mon pays est peu de chose mais, quand on est passablement quelque part, il faut y rester' (18:134-36). We must wait for Chapter 30 before we see a Candide ready and able to see any wisdom in that statement. Meanwhile, the travellers are free to go: 'tous les hommes sont libres' (18:138).

Leaving Eldorado proves to be as difficult as entering it, but the King commissions three thousand scientists to create an ingenious machine to ensure a safe exit, a testimony to the benefits of co-operative endeavour and collaboration that provides another link with Chapter 30. Accompanied by a hundred 'red sheep' loaded down with Eldoradan gold and precious stones, the 'deux vagabonds' (18:167) take their leave. Any authorial reproof implied by their new designation as 'vagabonds' is short-lived. Suggestions of greed and other morally dubious motives soon disappear, although the impression is left that neither Candide nor Cacambo was actually worthy of permanent residence in the city of gold (*16*, p.148).

On the other hand, significant changes for the better have taken place in the hero. From now on he will be able to break the freedom-denying links in the chain of cause-and-effect that has ordered his life in the pre-Eldoradan world of Optimism. Thoughts of Eldorado will not fade, moreover. In addition to their practical usefulness as living banks, the red sheep will perpetuate symbolically the presence of Eldorado in the rest of the *conte*. They will provide a splash of colour in the darkness, and remind Candide that all is never for the best, that there is always a better world, that solutions to some problems can be found, and that the human struggle against evil is not entirely futile. After Eldorado the paralysis of Optimism lifts a little; progress becomes a possibility, and the will to act manifests itself, freedom to act being assured by the contents of the bags carried by the red sheep.

6. *The Return*

Candide and Cacambo leave Eldorado rich and well-pleased
with themselves. Candide has reached a high point of happiness
and good fortune, and is elated with thoughts of Cunégonde
and of what he can do in Europe with his new-found wealth.
The first day of the journey back to Europe, and to the world as
it is, will take the travellers through the Dutch colony of
Surinam, and the prospects seem good (19:4-5). Silver linings
have clouds in *Candide*, however, and as Candide and
Cacambo move further away from Eldorado, their situation
deteriorates, and their reasons for complacency diminish.
Candide learns that wealth can disappear with distressing
rapidity as the red sheep start to die off, and eventually only
two remain. A chastened Candide takes refuge in dreams of
love, and Cacambo tries to lift his darkening mood with the
confident assurance that happiness still lies within their grasp
(19:17-18).

At this point, they are both brought up short by the sight
of a black slave, 'étendu par terre, n'ayant plus que la moitié de
son habit, c'est-à-dire d'un caleçon de toile bleue; il manquait à
ce pauvre homme la jambe gauche et la main droite' (19:19-
22). The description of the slave's degradation, with the
restrictive adverbials *ne . . .que, n'ayant plus que* exposing the
bare bones of his existence, present the reader once more with
the raw physicality of a human body in distress. This is no
magic-lantern silhouette, but a grimly realistic, non-caricatural
picture of a man in rags, lying on the ground with his left leg

and his right hand axed off. Voltaire's description of the slave's clothing and injuries draws accurately on the legislation concerning delinquent slaves set out in the 1685 *Code Noir*, updated in 1743 and not to be finally abolished until 1848.

The measured language and quasi-documentary tone of the description of the slave's appearance is juxtaposed with Candide's intensely emotional reaction. Unusually for *Candide*, narrative voice then blends with authorial voice as Candide recoils in horror and pity, and asks the slave what has reduced him to 'l'état horrible où je te vois' (19:22-24). In his answer, structured around the three eye-catching features, *caleçon, main,* and *jambe* already picked out at the start of the encounter, the slave explains his mutilations as everyday normalities, banalities (to him), and discounted with the use of the incongruously conversational *c'est que.* The nature of slavery, and what it means to be a slave, is communicated to the reader, not so much by what the slave says, but by how he says it. The true horror of the scene lies in the slave's fatalistic acceptance of his condition, qualities shared with the Optimists, a coincidence that will be brought out more explicitly in the next paragraph. Like all slaves, he waits, docile and compliant, for his master's instructions, the master in this case being Vanderdendur, 'le fameux négociant' (19:24-25). He accepts his treatment at the hands of the slaver, collaborating in his own degradation: 'c'est l'usage' (19:27-28). When slaves catch their fingers in the machinery at the sugar mill, he finds nothing remarkable in the requirement to have the whole hand amputated to avoid gangrene, or in the need to lose a leg when caught after an escape attempt. The details of the slave trade are set out in a matter-of-fact way, their impact on the reader maximised by the cold emptiness of the narrative voice used. There are as yet no mitigating cause/effect explanations, just the facts of human cruelty, of the law of the strong over the weak, of economic and colonial realities. All are illuminated against a contemporary backdrop of legal and metaphysical justifications of slavery from thinkers such as

Melon, Hobbes, Grotius and Pufendorf, and a *Code Noir* that
protected slaves as 'biens meubles'.

Voltaire's anger breaks through the cool surface of the
narrative as the slave then sums up the *raison suffisante* for his
situation; addressing Cacambo with a 'vous' that also
challenges the sugar-consuming reader to confront an evil, from
which Europe is benefiting and in which the reader might be
collaborating: 'C'est à ce prix que vous mangez du sucre en
Europe' (19:31-32). In this account of the scandal of slavery
Voltaire has captured a very modern awareness of the
compliant acquiescence of the condemned, their acceptance of
the outrages perpetrated on their bodies by their torturers and
executioners, and their readiness to absolve their tormentors
from responsibility for the cruelties inflicted. The slave's
helplessness and resignation are conveyed through the dulling
repetition of passive constructions: 'On nous donne un caleçon
de toile [. . .] on nous coupe la main [...] on nous coupe la
jambe [. . .]' (19:27, 29-31). A sequence of passive structures
emphasises the reduction of the slave to the status of object to
which unspeakable things can be done. The denial of his
humanity is completed with the comparison to dogs, monkeys
and parrots (19:38-39).

In the second half of the slave's speech, evil's companion
theme, Optimism, moves centre-stage. With the compensatory
'Cependant' (19:32) a terrible Panglossian balance is struck as
the evils of slavery are linked inescapably to the false
consolations of the 'cruel philosophy'. The slave recalls his
mother's homily on life after selling her son to the Dutch
colonisers. Slavish passivity and fatalism are not only to be
found on sugar plantations but are qualities also shared with
the slaves of Optimistic theory. Wherever Optimism flourishes,
the will to action and self-determination dies. The slave's
mother urges her son to appreciate the good effects that come
from apparently evil causes, to bless the colonising
missionaries, 'ils te feront vivre heureux', to accept his slavery,
'tu fais par là la fortune de ton père et de ta mère' (19:34-37).

Slavery becomes 'un honneur', and yet another 'proof' that all is for the best. With a resigned 'Hélas', the slave acknowledges that his life did not quite turn out as his mother predicted (19:37-45). Irony is subdued, but not entirely absent from this sober episode. The slave's articulate, sophisticated 'European' voice, and his use of learned terms like 'fétiches', 'prêcheurs' and 'généalogiste', offer unexpectedly eloquent testimony to a humanity denied to him by the fact of his enslavement.

As the evils of the slave-trade coalesce with those of the cruel philosophy, Candide addresses the absent Pangloss, excluding himself from the camp of the Optimists with a significant use of a possessive: 'Ô Pangloss! s'écria Candide, tu n'avais pas deviné cette abomination; c'en est fait, il faudra qu'à la fin je renonce à *ton* [my italics] optimisme' (19:46-48). Cacambo asks what Optimism is, depriving the noun of even the dignity of an article, and Candide regretfully dismisses Optimism with a withering aphorism: 'Hélas! [...] c'est la rage de soutenir que tout est bien quand on est mal' (19:49-50), his 'hélas' complementing that of the slave in the previous paragraph. He has taken the first steps towards self-determination and self-liberation. Sadly he must acknowledge that the mutilated negro is beyond help. He can only weep (as a sentimentalist) and move on (as an apprentice-pragmatist). In this defining moment of revelation and revolt, Candide and Cacambo enter the Surinam capital, and Voltaire winks mischievously at his reader-accomplice with a textual echo of Christ's entry into Jerusalem (19:50-51/Luke, 19:41-46).

On learning that Cunégonde is living in Buenos Aires as 'la maîtresse favorite de Monseigneur', and unable to go there to rescue her himself for fear of arrest on murder charges, Candide dispatches Cacambo with instructions to purchase Cunégonde's freedom, and join him in Venice. Cacambo applauds this 'sage résolution' and departs immediately: 'c'était un très bon homme que ce Cacambo' (19:78-79). To charter a ship bound for Europe Candide must negotiate with the merchant-slaver, Vanderdendur, who lives up to the promise of his name by cheating Candide out of his two remaining diamond-laden sheep. Charges laid against the slaver with a Dutch magistrate result in fruitless further expense, but no justice.

The affair shakes Candide's faith in human nature, and his mood blackens once more: 'La méchanceté des hommes se présentait à son esprit dans toute sa laideur' (19:119-23). He holds a competition to find a new companion to match his new mood, and to relieve the boredom of the forthcoming sea voyage to Europe. The problem of *ennui* will resurface in Chapter 25, and again in Chapter 29. As a result of the competition, Candide hopes to find 'un honnête homme [...] le plus dégoûté de son état et le plus malheureux de la province' (19:130-31), and he chooses Martin, a former proof-reader (21:15) in the Amsterdam book-trade, and a suspected Socinian. Martin's background suggests that Bayle might not have been far from Voltaire's mind. With Martin's appointment, Candide will start to take account of the claims of an alternative system to that of Pangloss.

The High Seas

During the sea voyage from Surinam to Bordeaux, via the Cape of Good Hope and Japan – a world tour whose scope and bizarre itinerary ironically escape the hero's notice, Candide and Martin have plenty of time to reflect on events, and to rehearse the arguments about moral and physical evil from the new angle of Martin's bleak Manicheism. Manichean doctrine, a Christian heresy established in the third century by Manes, envisaged the creation of the universe as the work of two co-equal forces of good and evil, evil being the force responsible for the creation of our own world. This let God off the hook as far as responsibility for evil is concerned, but it denied God omnipotence (8, p.98). Voltaire was still flirting with Manicheism as late as 1764 in *Le Blanc et le noir*, but ultimately found it too harsh a doctrine.

Martin is nevertheless portrayed in a less flamboyantly satirical way than Pangloss, his Hobbesian vision of a human condition in which evil predominates being a little closer to the facts. Candide's advantage over his new companion is made clear from the start, however: 'L'un et l'autre avaient beaucoup vu et beaucoup souffert [...] Cependant Candide avait un grand avantage sur Martin, c'est qu'il espérait toujours revoir mademoiselle Cunégonde, et que Martin n'avait rien à espérer' (20:2-3, 7-9). Martin, moreover, like Pangloss, makes mis-judgments, as in the case of Cacambo. Hope in Chapter 20 is admittedly based on a dream of love that will prove ultimately to be illusory, but it is no less valid for that as a factor in the hero's survival, and it nurtures his will to carry on. In a letter written to Bertrand in 1756, where Voltaire denounced the false consolations of the cruel philosophy, he also observed that *bien* in the Leibnizian formula, 'tout est bien', connoted *mieux* (D6738), although the Optimists would never admit it.

Philosophising with Martin involves genuine dialogue, not a one-way flow of dogma. Candide, in spite of some persistent traces of nostalgia for Panglossian placebos, encouraged by a full stomach and thoughts of Cunégonde (20:14-15), is now a sceptical interlocutor of system-builders. His challenge to Martin does not, however, involve the latter's satirical demolition. Martin's Manicheism may in the end be as wrong as Pangloss's Optimism, but Martin is not foolishly wrong, and his views are accorded a serious hearing. As far as evil is concerned, Martin can at least argue on the basis of evidence and, if we leave his blind spot regarding Cacambo aside, his system is predicated on what his senses tell him. He deduces from his observations that God has abandoned the world to the devil, with the exception of Eldorado, for which he must take Candide's word. Martin's own experience, and what he knows of Candide's, suggests that life amounts to little more than the pursuit of mutual destruction in a world in which the powerful treat the weak as sheep for slaughter, in which Europe is at the mercy of 'assassins enrégimentés', and in which human nature is shaped only by malice, greed and envy. To Candide's objection, 'Il y a pourtant du bon' (20:42), Martin's reply is sceptical: 'Cela peut être [...] mais je ne le connais pas'. Candide's interrogation of Martin reflects his evolution, the beginnings of wisdom and a growing ability to learn from experience.

As always during philosophical exchanges in *Candide*, plot developments provide an evaluative gloss on what has been said. Martin's world-view seems to gain support from this quarter as a naval battle breaks out, and a ship sinks with the loss of a hundred lives. Candide is compelled to accept the presence of 'quelque chose de diabolique dans cette affaire' (20:56-57). He now accepts that evil is omnipresent, and he will be increasingly concerned from now on with the way to avoid the consequences of this acknowledged fact. The way forward is signposted symbolically when he spots through his telescope a splash of bright red in the heaving seas. This turns out to be one of the two stolen red sheep, still the bearer of his diamonds and, by symbolic extension, hope and echoes of the parable of the lost sheep (Matthew, 18:13-14).

The sinking ship is the Dutch pirate vessel carrying Vanderdendur, and the justice denied to Candide in Surinam is now granted. The survival of the last of the red sheep is enough for Candide to resist the attractions of Martin's philosophy. Like the Good Shepherd, Candide 'eut plus de joie de retrouver ce mouton qu'il n'avait été affligé d'en perdre cent tous chargés de gros diamants d'Eldorado' (20:60-62). Voltaire takes care to avoid the trap of conceding a *tout est au mieux* implication, however, with Martin's riposte: Did innocent passengers have to die as well? God has punished the guilty Vanderdendur, perhaps, but the devil has drowned the others (20:70-72). The question is unanswerable, and in the end metaphysical speculation loses its power over Candide and becomes just a way of passing the time during the remaining fifteen days of the journey.

No further details about their discussions are given, except for the fact that 'au bout de quinze jours ils étaient aussi avancés que le premier' (20:75-76). Above all, Martin and Candide 'se consolaient'. Martin is important to Candide, not for philosophical reasons but for reasons relating to human solidarity, so prized by Voltaire in the *Poème sur le désastre de Lisbonne*. Martin offers a friendship enriched by the shared experience of suffering. His Manicheism engages Candide's attention for the duration of the voyage, but unlike his earlier self he no longer believes 'innocently' in what he is told. The retrieval of the lost sheep ensures that words and systems can no longer imprison him. The red sheep, with its Eldoradan associations and its valuable cargo, means that the quest for the future can continue, and in the face of systems that threaten paralysis, hope prevails and events can still be determined by the action of individuals: 'Candide caressait son mouton. «Puisque je t'ai retrouvé, dit-il, je pourrai bien retrouver Cunégonde»' (20:78-79).

Meanwhile, philosophy can amuse, when there is nothing better to do. As the ship reaches its destination, a final, desultory exchange takes place, its irrelevance pointed up ironically with an 'A propos' with which Candide teases Martin about the origins of the earth (21:32-33). Candide's line of questioning reveals new signs of an enquiring mind, but Martin wisely refuses the invitation to indulge in further 'rêveries', and his reply to a second question about the purpose of creation is confined to a terse comment in the style of the dervish in Chapter 30: 'Pour nous faire enrager'. Further attempts to explore issues relating to human nature, the implications of the loveplay between the apes and the Oreillon girls, observed by Candide and Cacambo in Chapter 16, the nature of man and the vexed Rousseauist issue of the origins of man's wickedness (2:39-44) serve only to demonstrate that Pessimists, like Optimists, have systems predicated for different reasons on a static view of nature and human nature. Neither system can accommodate the dynamic possibilities of choice, control and change. For Martin, as for Hobbes, human beings are no more capable of changing their predatory ways than sparrowhawks, and he opts in the end for a predeterminism as uncompromising as that of Pangloss.

The discussion peters out inconclusively with a half-finished sentence from Candide about free-will, and the ship, unaffected, like the world itself, by systems and words, sails on to Bordeaux where the captain brings it safely to harbour. The ship on which Candide booked his return to Europe has charted an orderly, purposeful course determined by human will and human ingenuity, not by chance or by providential design. The Candide-Martin exchange has been a game, useful only as a diversion from the boredom of the voyage, as Candide anticipated when he chose Martin to be his companion. With Bordeaux in sight, the game terminates, 'en raisonnant ainsi' (21:50).

France

Candide's journey from Bordeaux to Venice is complicated by two detours. The first is to Paris, undertaken out of curiosity to discover whether the city can live up to its reputation. The second involves an even more circuitous diversion northwards to Dieppe and a trip across the Channel to Portsmouth harbour, where Candide witnesses the Byng execution.

After leaving his one remaining sheep with the Bordeaux Academy of Sciences, whose prize in the competition to discover the reason for the sheep's redness has been awarded to 'un savant du Nord', an allusion to Maupertuis (22:8-10), Candide and Martin set off for Paris. They enter the city through the southern suburbs by the faubourg Saint-Marceau, and Candide's high expectations are soon dashed with his first glimpse of a city which reminds him of the worst village in Westphalia (22:14-15). Paris is the place where parasites live on wealth produced by the work others, a location of *ennui, vice* and *besoin* that soon makes Candide feel ill. His illness affords a

somewhat artificial opportunity for conventionally satirical digs
at the commercialism of Parisian doctors and clerics. Martin
notes how the possession of wealth is in direct ratio to the
degree of warmth in a Parisian welcome, and remembers his
own rather different experience of Paris in harder times (22:23-
26). Convalescing after his illness, Candide is entertained by a
new crowd of friends scenting easy pickings. He is persuaded to
play cards and to his surprise, but not Martin's, is cheated by
cardsharpers.

The narrative now assumes the flavour of a *roman
d'initiation*. A guide to Paris offers his services in the form of a
slimy ecclesiastic, 'un petit abbé périgourdin', who first of all
takes the two travellers to the theatre. Candide finds himself
sitting next to fault-finding critics who spoil his enjoyment of a
play set 'en Arabie', written by a person 'qui ne croit pas aux
idées innées' (22:55-56), by pulling to pieces the performance
of the actors – possibly an allusion to the hostile reception of
Voltaire's own *Orphelin de la Chine* in 1755. It is at this point
that the substantial block of text added in 1761 starts. Candide
is particularly taken with an actress who reminds him of
Cunégonde, and asks how actresses are regarded in Paris. He is
told that Parisians revere living actresses, but throw their bodies
into the sewers when they die. This prompts Martin to recall
the burial of 'Mlle Monime' (22:74-79). Monime is the name
of the heroine of Racine's *Mithridate*, a role played by the
beautiful Adrienne Lecouvreur who, like all members of the
acting profession, unless they recanted, had been buried in
unconsecrated ground – an incident that had haunted Voltaire
since 1730.

A series of portraits followed by acerbic counter-portraits
reversing Candide's naïve first impressions of Paris now follows
(22:50-96), echoing parodically Montesquieu's question and
answer technique in the salon scene in Letter 48 of the *Lettres
persanes*. The portraits are all of contemporaries, including an
enemy, the journalist Fréron, editor of the *Année littéraire*, and
Mlle Clairon, another well-known actress who had performed

in Voltaire's *Tancrède* in 1760, and with whom Candide would like to dine, 'quoique je sois très empressé de revoir mademoiselle Cunégonde' (22:99-101). The abbé offers instead to arrange a dinner with another 'dame de qualité', and takes Candide to a house in the rue Saint-Honoré where, in one of the more memorable scenes in this chapter, he observes the silent tensions of a gambling den where games of *pharaon* (a kind of baccarat) are presided over by the lynx-eyed 'marquise' de Parolignac, assisted by 'un banquier impitoyable', and alerted by the facial signals of her daughter to any cheating on the part of the *pontes*, or punters (22:111-20). After Candide has been relieved of fifty thousand francs, suffering his losses with a *sang-froid* that makes the lackeys think he is an English milord, the scene dissolves seamlessly into the false gaiety and din of a supper party. The supper is a further occasion for initiating Candide into the ways of Paris by means of another set of satirical portraits of two more of Voltaire's enemies, Gauchat and Trublet (22:133-75).

The corruption, pleasures and perversions of French 'civilisation' are explored in a long, finely etched sequence of scenes which interferes less with the tale's overall thematic coherence than has sometimes been suggested. Conversation at the dinner table soon turns to Pangloss, which helps to keep the chapter positioned within the overall frame of reference to Optimism. Although Pangloss is formally absent from the scene, his interrogation continues by proxy in the form of a conversation with a 'savant' whom Candide mistakenly takes at first for 'un autre Pangloss' (22:185). The 'savant', however, is no believer in Leibnizio-Wolffian order and, like Martin, sees only chaos and disorder. Society is just war by other means, 'une guerre éternelle' (22:188-98). Candide's appeal to the authority of another 'savant', now hanged, who taught him 'que tout cela est à merveille', lacks conviction. Drawing on Leibniz's *Théodicée* directly, Candide makes one of his last defences of providentialism with a description of evil phenomena as 'des ombres à un beau tableau' (22:201). The despairing pessimism of the chaos theorist appeals to Martin, who observes that the shadows are in fact horrible stains. The first half of Candide's response echoes Rousseau and the second half Pangloss: 'Ce sont les hommes qui font les taches [...] et ils ne peuvent pas s'en dispenser' (22:204-05). Martin draws out the implication: men cannot therefore be responsible for their actions, 'ce n'est pas donc leur faute'. Martin and the 'savant' continue to debate abstractions while the gamblers, 'qui n'entendaient rien à ce langage', drink on.

Candide turns away from philosophy to sexual banter, and eventually sexual congress, with Mme de Parolignac in a scene of commercial sex that evokes initially a mocking replay of the handkerchief-dropping ploy in Chapter 1. Thoughts of Cunégonde vanish, however, with startling lack of resistance on Candide's part as the 'marquise' inflames his lust, and disarms his conscience. With a casual act of infidelity, Voltaire neatly ensures that the hero stains the 'beau tableau' of his own sentimental ideals of courtly love and chivalry. The brothel scene has displayed the hero at the mercy of his sensuality, but his lapse does not distract him from the quest for Cunégonde. He assures his sly Parisian guide 'qu'il demanderait bien pardon à cette belle de son infidélité, quand il la verrait à Venise' (22:237-38). This marks the end of the 1761 insertion.

Neither the reassertion of his will nor the dawning awareness of the place of human responsibility and action in the good-evil equation, has yet armed Candide invincibly against the ways of the world or the siren words of Pangloss, as the strange incident of the 'false Cunégonde' illustrates. The 'abbé périgourdin', with his eye always to the main chance, exploits Candide's anxiety to see his lover again, and forges a love-letter supposedly written by the heroine (22:259-65). Counterfeit love is shown to be indistinguishable from the real thing, at least on paper, and Candide agrees to an assignation in a hotel bedroom where the abbé's accomplice, the false Cunégonde, is waiting silently behind the drawn curtains of a four-poster. Candide is convinced by the charade that he is in

the presence of the heroine. The darker side of the Paris of the
late 1750s is now unveiled. As Candide pours tears and
diamonds into the false Cunégonde's outstretched hand poking
through the curtains, the police arrive with the abbé-informer.
Candide and Martin are arrested, 'au milieu de ces transports',
as suspect foreigners, and dragged off to prison (22:280-87).

Voltaire has now entered dangerous waters. In a much
re-worked paragraph he depicts the hysteria reigning in France
in the wake of the assassination attempt on Louis XV's life by
Robert Damiens, delicately referred to as 'un gueux du pays
d'Atrébatie' (22:307), 'Atrébatie' being the latinised form for
the Artois, birthplace of the cruelly executed Damiens. The
oblique reference to regicide is reinforced with supplementary
allusions to the attempt on Henri IV's life in 1594, and to his
actual assassination in 1610. The Damiens incident was still
dangerous to talk or write about in 1761, and the matter is
swiftly subsumed into the flow of narrative events as Candide
acts to survive the lethal xenophobia unleashed in Paris in the
aftermath of this event. Eldoradan wealth again provides the
means to turn the will to act into the freedom to act. The police
chief is bought off, and helps Candide and Martin to escape 'au
plus vite de ce pays où des singes agacent des tigres' (22:315-
16). Their escape-route will take them first of all to Dieppe and
Portsmouth, not the most direct route to Venice and to
Cunégonde, but at least a deliverance from the jaws of Hell
that had now opened in the land of art and culture, 'chez un
peuple qui danse et qui chante' (22:314-15, 326-28).

Italy (via England)

The last lap of the journey to Venice reacquaints Candide
briefly with the events of the Seven Years' War when he
witnesses a different form of national madness with the
execution of John Byng, the English admiral executed on 14
March 1757 for dereliction of duty in not engaging effectively
with Admiral Galissonnière's fleet at the Battle of Minorca. In

this memorable cameo an unnamed man, blindfolded and on his knees, takes twelve shots to the head from a four-man firing squad, to the great satisfaction of the watching crowd (23:16-19). The occasion is also an opportunity for Voltaire to remind readers of the Seven Years' War side-show in Quebec, and the futility of a war over 'quelques arpents de neige vers le Canada' (23:7).

The terms in which Candide's question to the crowd is framed reflects Martin's view of evil's dominion: 'Qu'est-ce donc que tout ceci? [...] et quel démon exerce partout son empire?' (23:21). The crowd does not know the victim. As with the slaughtered soldiers and civilians in Chapter 3, and the impaled heads in Constantinople in Chapter 29, anonymity, legal sanction and a splash of ceremony imbue the official atrocity against Byng with a spurious sense of order and *tout est au mieux* legitimacy, depriving the scene of all vestige of justice and morality, and the victim himself of human reality and individuality. Byng remains throughout unidentified, just 'un assez gros homme' (23:15-16). Nobody else in the scene is named, apart from Candide and Martin, and the reiterative use of the passive *on* accentuates the anonymity of the participants and their callous indifference, perhaps for Voltaire the worst consequence of all of Optimism: 'qu'on venait de tuer [...] lui répondit-on [...] lui dit-on [...] on a trouvé [...]' (23:22-28). Candide learns eventually that the man lying on the deck with the shattered skull is just another admiral, sentenced to death for not killing enough people. Optimism now touches England with the calculation that the benefits to naval discipline will outweigh the partial evil of the atrocity: 'il est bon de tuer de temps en temps un amiral pour encourager les autres' (23:29-30).

The Byng execution in Portsmouth harbour was the nearest that Voltaire got in *Candide* to associating England with the 'cruel philosophy'. Not even the civilised social and political features of English life can eradicate man's insane predilection for cruelty and inhumanity, a theme in this chapter that recalls modern reflections on the paradox of Nazism's birth in the cradle of European high culture. In sharp contrast to his conduct in the earlier scenes of war, Candide does not turn away from the grim events taking place before him. No Optimistic consolations spring automatically to his lips, although he will lapse again into Optimistic formulations as soon as he thinks of Cunégonde and Cacambo waiting for him in Venice. He resolves not to set foot in England. Byng, like the mutilated negro, can be pitied but not helped, and Candide can only look hopefully and pragmatically to the future.

The Italian experience covers three substantial chapters (24-26), and the carnival itself invites comparison with the carnival of life (*26*, pp.651-52). The scenes set in Venice also provide a test-bed for Manichean pessimism which crystallises around the question of the reappearance of 'le bon Cacambo' (*29*, pp.114-15). Candide's faith in human nature *malgré tout*, expressed in his confident belief that Cacambo will be waiting for him in Venice with Cunégonde, as instructed, has been continually eroded by Martin's scepticism about Cacambo's motives. At the start of Chapter 24 Candide concedes that Martin's jaundiced view of Cacambo might well be justified when neither Cacambo nor Cunégonde materialises as planned. As a result, Candide falls temporarily into 'une mélancolie noire' (24:16) that numbs him to the delights of the Venice carnival. Martin reproaches him for naïvety in thinking that a valet would not abscond with the money and the girl, and advises him to forget both. Martin is no longer a source of consolation, and Candide's despair deepens as the Manichean 'proves' that there is little virtue and happiness in the world, 'excepté peut-être dans Eldorado, où personne ne pouvait aller' (24:25-28).

Despite his fears for the worst, Candide challenges the notion that happiness is not attainable. Seeking evidence to counter Martin's nihilism, he seizes on the apparent happiness of a passing monk with a girl on his arm, and invites the couple to dinner. A surprise recognition scene ensues in which the girl turns out to be Paquette, the servant from Thunder-ten-Tronckh, and source of Pangloss's syphilis. However, Paquette and the young monk, Giroflée, cannot provide Candide with the evidence that he needs, but their account of 'malheurs épouvantables' does not undermine his challenge. After Paquette's tale of catastrophe, followed by Giroflée's sad story, Martin claims victory: 'Eh bien [...] n'ai-je pas gagné la gageure tout entière?' (24:125-26). Candide responds with a Jacques-like action: he offers the two unfortunates money, insisting that with practical help happiness will follow. As Martin expresses futher doubts on that score, Candide reviews the empirical evidence for hope, to which Pangloss and Martin both represent a threat: 'je vois qu'on retrouve souvent les gens qu'on ne croyait jamais retrouver; il se pourra bien faire qu'ayant rencontré mon mouton rouge et Paquette, je rencontre aussi Cunégonde'. Martin remains unimpressed: 'C'est que j'ai vécu' (24:131-36).

In spite of Martin's *chute* as a systemiser, the Manichean position for the Voltaire of the 1750s was not a target for easy satirical dismissal. A serious exchange between Candide and Martin on the possibilities for human happiness is thus allowed to run freely through Chapter 25, in which the jaded disillusionment of the Venetian nobleman Pococuranté is explored, and through Chapter 26, in which the quest for happiness through the exercise of power is tested to destruction with the story of the six kings.

The approach to Pococuranté's palace and the Venetian nobleman's reception of Candide and Martin are reminiscent of the scenes of hospitality at the court of the King of Eldorado. Pococuranté's estate has luxuriously ornamental gardens, pleasing architecture, an elegant, attractive and seemingly happy entourage of servants. It is a location of lavish wealth and conspicuous consumption (25:1-17). Pococuranté should be happy, but he is eaten away by *ennui*. The trappings of wealth, the benefits of art, theatre and poetry have little to offer but boredom, lassitude and a disaffection with life which seems to get worse as the tour of Pococuranté's house and garden progresses. Nothing pleases, everything palls. As Candide already knows, and as Voltaire himself discovered at an early stage in his life, economic well-being is a prerequisite for survival and security. However, Candide is not allowed in the end to have too much material wealth. To retreat from the world into sybaritic indolence is never an option for him, and the zest for survival is thereby sustained. The best of all possible economic worlds denies Pococuranté a goal and a purpose. Pococuranté has no story to tell, and Voltaire reminds us in this episode that the spiritual vacuum of unhappiness is not necessarily the consequence of external forces, but can also come from within.

For Pococuranté even literature, art and music offer few attractions. His collection of works by the world's great writers seems to be part of a cultural graveyard rather than a working library. Above all, there is no work for him to do. Pococuranté's fate is to be terminally idle, disengaged from the collective human struggle against evil, a sterile product of his class. He has a garden, but it is not being cultivated productively by his own efforts (25:150-54), although we are told he is going to work at it the next day. It is also possible to see in the portrayal of Pococuranté a measure of authorial self-interrogation perhaps (*24*, p.64). The reader will be reminded of the flaws in Pococuranté's garden in the concluding chapter of the *conte*.

At the end of the meeting with the Venetian *sénateur*, Candide, still anxious to counter Martin's views, tries to draw positive conclusions about Pococuranté's life (25:156-64), but Martin has the last word, and Candide is obliged to fall back on Cunégonde for proof of the existence of happiness in the world. In response, Martin offers an aphorism which, like the aphorism about *bienfaisance* placed in the mouth of the recruiter in Chapter 2, has a double-edged irony. In the context of the scene the speaker implies the contrary to what he is saying, but in the context of the *conte* as a whole there is a positive implication in which the irony works against the speaker: 'C'est toujours bien fait d'espérer, dit Martin' (25:164-66).

The supper with the six kings in the next chapter, another carnivalesque tableau (*26*; *22*, p.93), starts with a narrative reinforcement of Candide's faith in human nature. The occasion for the triumph of hope over despair in this context comes when Candide feels a tap on his shoulder and sees Cacambo, 'son agent fidèle', whose reappearance in Venice now justifies Candide's resistance to Martin's scepticism. Martin is silent, and Candide's joy at finding his quadroon again is tempered only by the news that Cunégonde is not in Venice, but in Constantinople (26:1-10).

Before embarking on the last stage of the journey Candide and Martin must first listen to the tales of the six strangers. In this strangely ritualistic scene all six are historical figures, kings who have lost their thrones, and who can testify to the fragility and precariousness of kingly power, and of the principle of political authority itself (*26*, pp.651-62): Sultan Achmet III (1673-1736), deposed by his nephew Mahmoud I in 1730; Czar Ivan VI (1740-64), deposed by Elizabeth and later strangled on the orders of Catherine the Great; Bonny Prince Charlie, the Young Pretender (1720-88), defeated at Culloden in 1746; Augustus III (1696-1763), Elector of Saxony and King of Poland, defeated by Frederick the Great in 1756; Stanislas I (1677-1766), reduced to the dukedom of Lorraine in 1735 where he often invited Voltaire to his court at Lunéville, and the elected King Theodore of Corsica (1670-1756), imprisoned in London for debt. All of these topical examples of failed kingship have experienced the ephemeral nature of high rank, their disempowerment and demotion brilliantly evoked in the plaintive refrain with which each cautionary tale closes: 'et je suis venu passer le carnaval à Venise'. These six crowned heads of Europe are silhouettes, shadow-symbols of dispossession and political disorder, relegated unceremoniously to the chorus-line of history (26:49-89).

The theatre-of-life scenes in Venice reveal a Candide convinced that happinesss is possible, but alerted to the dangers of basing happiness on wealth and power alone. The distress of five of the kings is increased in an interesting incident at this point, prefiguring the political and economic implications of the new order that will emerge in Candide's garden. After giving money to the impoverished ex-King Theodore, the kings are presented with evidence of the economic muscle of the rising *bourgeoisie* when Candide, 'ce simple particulier', bestows on King Theodore a lavish gift of diamonds and jewels (26:91-95). After giving handouts to royalty, Candide now loses interest in kings, and the arrival of yet another batch of dethroned 'altesses sérénissimes' barely registers (26:100-01).

7. Conclusion: Candide's Garden

The last two chapters of *Candide* have been the subject of an astonishingly wide range of critical comment, and much disagreement. The definitive interpretation of *Candide*'s conclusion still remains elusive up to a point, although the exhortation to cultivate the garden does not quite match the opaqueness of endings to other Voltairean *contes* such as the blank page in the Book of Knowledge in *Micromégas*, or the ellipsis following Zadig's insistent 'Mais' (*29*, pp.121-23). In the last twenty years, structuralist and post-structuralist methodologies, and particularly the narratological methods distinguishing between *récit* and *discours* pioneered by Genette, Greimas and others, as well as more traditional, positivist approaches, have greatly enriched our understanding, not only of what the conclusion *means,* but of how it *works* in the context of the symbolic codes and formal structures of the tale.

The chapter-heading describes Chapter 30 simply as a 'Conclusion', inviting the reader to expect an ending and a resolution. The resolution has been carefully prepared throughout the *conte,* and materialises explicitly in the three chapters preceding the conclusion. In Chapter 27 Cacambo has assured Candide that Cunégonde is alive but reduced to washing dishes in the waters of what is now known as the Sea of Marmora, for Ragotski, the Prince of Transylvania, who in real life had taken refuge in Turkey in 1719. Candide is warned that his lover has become horribly ugly; and answers presciently: 'Ah! belle ou laide [...] je suis honnête homme, et mon devoir est de l'aimer toujours' (27:30-31). Much of the money given to Cacambo has been spent on purchasing

Cunégonde's freedom, as part of a job lot with the Old
Woman, from the Governor of Buenos Aires, and the rest has
been lost to a pirate.

In spite of these 'épouvantables calamités enchaînées les
unes aux autres', Candide resolves to break the enslaving chain
of fate. The few remaining Eldoradan diamonds will ensure
Cunégonde's final deliverance, in spite of the disappointing
news about her physical deterioration. Cacambo's freedom is
purchased immediately, and they set off in a slave-galley for
Propontis to meet up with the heroine, 'quelque laide qu'elle
pût être' (27:60-61). Repeated reference to Cunégonde's
ugliness marks the start of Candide's awakening from the
dream of romantic love and hints at the new realities ahead.
The cast for the final curtain-call gathers as Pangloss and the
death-defying Baron's son resurface as galley-slaves, and
Martin and Pangloss meet for the first time. Pretensions and
realities clash again as Candide asks the galley-commandant
how much he wants for 'Monsieur de Thunder-ten-Tronckh,
un des premiers barons de l'Empire, et [...] Monsieur Pangloss,
le plus profond métaphysicien d'Allemagne' (27:85-88). The
levanti patron, to whom such grandiose titles mean nothing,
agrees to the sale of 'deux chiens de forçats chrétiens' for fifty
thousand gold coins, a ransom that Candide raises by selling
diamonds to Jews upon arrival at Constantinople.

Pangloss has been ravaged by syphilis, hanged, dissected,
infected, blinded, thrashed and sentenced to the galleys. He
continues to insist that all is still for the best, but his defence of
the cruel philosophy is now formulated defensively, and with a
hint of self-apology, as he takes refuge from empirical
objections, not in philosophical argument, but in the demands
imposed by his professional duties. It is here in Pangloss's last
major defence of Optimism, in which his own experience
provides the ironic counter-evidence, that Leibniz is mentioned
for the first time by name (28:78-79).

The din of Leibnizio-Wolffian catchwords reaches a
crescendo at the start of Chapter 29. Pangloss, freed from the

slavery of galley service, remains in servitude to his own logical 'enchaînements', and to that paralysing fatalism linked inescapably to Leibnizian metaphysics. 'Raisonnements' continue until Candide, Pangloss, Martin, Cacambo and the Baron's son reach the house of the Prince of Transylvania near Constantinople, where they find Cunégonde and the Old Woman drying the Prince's washing. The chivalric quest for the heroine ends with a final burlesque flourish in an open-air laundry. Love has been purged of its fabulous accretions, and especially of (male) optimistic dreams and expectations (*13*, p.89). A parallel reunion of Pangloss and Paquette is marked by a similar, though in Pangloss's case temporary, outbreak of realism (30:65-69).

The long-awaited narrative climax of the lovers' reunion is unceremoniously deflated, the shocking physical reality of Cunégonde displacing with precisely arranged symmetry the terms of her description in Chapter 1 (*14*). Unlike Candide, she has aged. As with her companion, the Old Woman, the early promise of youth and beauty has delivered only misfortune. Candide, still the 'tendre amant' (29:11), recoils in horror, in spite of his earlier good intentions, and even Cunégonde's brother pales at the sight. Cunégonde has undergone other changes too, reflected in her response to her lover's unexpected arrival. The disruptively lusty farce of the first (interrupted) kiss in Chapter 1 is now replaced by a sober, unsentimental scene of reunion, its emotional content restricted to a simple, honest gesture of affection (29:14-15). The scene is presented without literary adornment, and there is no trace of the sardonic tone and coarse hilarity of the fumbling, ill-fated tryst in the Baron's castle.

The values of human solidarity mitigating the pain of lost dreams, are promoted once again when the Old Woman persuades Candide to buy a nearby small-holding 'en attendant que toute la troupe eût une meilleure destinée' (29:18-19). Candide buys the land with the last of his diamonds, once more demonstrating the economic realities upon which from now on

his power and authority will be exercised – another contrastive
parallel with the hollow claims made in Chapter 1 by the
Baron, and perpetuated in the last paragraph of Chapter 29 by
the Baron's son. Wealth is useful and facilitates action and
progress, but is no solution in itself, as the encounter with
Pococuranté has demonstrated. Moreover, it has a tendency to
disappear, its ephemeral nature having become only too clear in
the episodes describing Candide's losses at the hands of
Vanderdendur (19:89-111), Jewish usurers (7:106-09, 30:20)
and card-sharpers (22:127-29). However, Candide is allowed
to retain something, and the importance of his diamonds as a
contributory factor in the tale's resolution should not be
discounted. This is reinforced by their continuing association
with the red sheep of Eldorado.

Some of the principles upon which Candide's garden will
be predicated are now falling into place. Power based on the
privileges of rank alone is thinly disguised impotence. In the
Chapter 1/Chapter 30 diptych money-based power is taken out
of aristocratic hands, and relocated in those of the *bourgeoisie*,
a transfer already dramatised in the encounter with the six kings
in Chapter 26. At the end of the *conte* the world changes for
Cunégonde, the Old Woman, Pangloss, Martin (but not the
Baron's son), and the *enchaînement* of a class-based hierarchy of
pre-established social and political order is dismantled. The
world changes for Candide in part because of his economic
status: he can purchase the freedom of his friends; he can buy
the land for his garden which could not have come into
existence without the resources, in the form of diamonds and
ideals, of Eldorado.

Cunégonde is unaware of her ugliness, but her state of
happy ignorance is charitably preserved by the group: 'personne
ne l'en avait avertie' (29:19-20). If the chivalric dream of love
dies, honour, loyalty and duty survive. 'Le bon Candide' is
reminded of his earlier commitment and professions of
affection, and he keeps his promise to marry his dilapidated
lover, or more precisely '[il] n'osa pas la refuser' (20:22). In a

significantly modified replay of events in Chapter 1, the Baron's son, unchanged and unchangeable, raises traditional objections to the marriage of Candide to his sister. With the Baron's son, *ancien régime* class privilege, the world of the feudal past to which, in the case of the castle, a torch had already been put, lives on. This time, however, an autocratic kick can no longer resolve matters. As part of the unreconstructed past, the Baron's son has no place in Candide's future. Unable to learn from history, he must be returned to it, and condemned to relive it.

The moribund world of Thunder-ten-Tronckh thus makes its last appearance in *Candide*, and the manner of its demise casts further light on the operating principles behind the new 'royaume' about to be born. The question mark placed originally over the Leibnizian order is now placed over the social and political order, signalled with the use of the egalitarian 'tu' in Candide's angry response threatening the baron's son with a second death. Having referred to Candide as 'vous' in their exchanges so far, the Baron's son responds to the bold familiarity in similar style deferring, at least grammatically, to a different order of social exchange (29:29-34).

The young Baron's 'impertinence' strengthens Candide's determination to marry Cunégonde, although he does not really relish the prospect (30:1-2). The Baron's son is a Jesuit as well as an aristocrat in the chevalier de Rohan mould, and as such he represents two pillars of the *ancien régime* that Voltaire hated. Nevertheless, too much political significance should not be read into the expulsion scene (*24*, pp.52-53), and it should always be remembered that Voltaire never preached revolution. In fact, he feared its advent. Political points are being made nevertheless. Candide decides his adversary's fate only after consultation with Pangloss, Martin and Cacambo (30:5-11), in marked contrast to the arbitrary circumstances of Candide's own expulsion in Chapter 1. At this point, Pangloss makes his first useful contribution, proving in 'un beau mémoire' that the Jesuit-Baron has no legal hold over Cunégonde. He devises a technical solution for the marriage to go ahead 'selon toutes les lois de l'Empire'. The principle of legitimacy now supplements that of equality in the new order of Candide's garden.

Having consigned the Baron/Jesuit and the feudal world to history, Candide and his companions must now face the future. Events are recapitulated, and the tensions between Optimism and Pessimism, hope and despair, sentimentalism and pragmatism, theory and experience, lies and truth, are woven together in a final distillation of the common predicament. For the first time, except for the Eldoradan episode, tranquillity reigns, the lovers are reunited, bodies have ceased to bleed, tyranny has been banished, and the basic conditions for what happiness there is in this world are in place. Human resilience at the physical and spiritual level, not to mention the indomitable human will to survive, have triumphed. Together with the *fact* of survival, this is probably the strongest narrative clue that all is not lost in *Candide*'s vale of tears. At this juncture, however, bad-tempered self-pity casts its shadow, and the door to the future still seems to be closed. Candide has been cheated by Jews, Cunégonde grows uglier and more cantankerous by the day, and the Old Woman is even more bad-tempered.

Cacambo, on the other hand, is working the land, and selling produce to nearby Constantinople. His productive example is an obvious prelude to Candide's. But cultivation in Cacambo's prototype garden is a solitary, negative activity, with little personal reward or sense of fulfilment (*16*, p.110). Cacambo finds work exhausting and curses his fate (30:23-24). This is the work required of Adam by a vengeful God after the Fall, and will be supplanted by the co-operative blessings of work in another garden, to be orchestrated by another Adam without the assistance of the deity. For the moment, however, Cacambo and the others are passing through what is in effect a secular Purgatory. Pangloss wishes to be elsewhere, preferably a shining star in some German University, while Martin waits stoically for the worst to happen. Outside, the world is still as dangerous as ever. Political turmoil rages in Constantinople, and boatloads of exiles are seen on the way to island-prisons. The impaled heads of the executed are a visible reminder that there are no safe havens, and the spectacle inspires further desultory philosophising, interspersed with deep feelings of the boredom already flagged as a threat to happiness in the Pococuranté episode.

The Old Woman draws up the balance-sheet of their misfortunes, and presents Candide with the bottom line: 'Je voudrais savoir lequel est le pire, ou d'être violée cent fois par des pirates nègres, [...] d'éprouver enfin toutes les misères par lesquelles nous avons tous passé, ou bien de rester ici à ne rien faire?' (30:39-44). Candide accepts her analysis, but refuses to speculate further. His response to Martin's renewed conviction that man is doomed to live in 'les convulsions de l'inquiétude, ou dans la léthargie de l'ennui' (30:47-48) is non-committal. Pangloss's reaction is interesting. He now acknowledges that he has suffered horribly, 'mais, ayant soutenu une fois que tout allait à merveille, il le soutenait toujours et n'en croyait rien' (30:49-52). The arrival of Paquette and Giroflée, 'dans la plus extrême misère' leads Martin to reprimand Candide in an unappealingly triumphalist tone for his refusal to accept explicitly that all is for the worst (30:61-65). Martin's principles are now 'détestables', and again Pangloss's explanation for events is restrained, and culminates in an uncharacteristic exclamation: 'Et qu'est-ce que ce monde!' (30:68-69).

Philosophical activity reaches new heights, and the decision is taken to consult a dervish, 'qui passait pour le meilleur philosophe de la Turquie' (30:71-72). The dervish cuts off Pangloss's speculative inquiry about the purpose of human life with curt advice not to meddle in such matters. Candide's factual observation, 'Mais [. . .] il y a horriblement de mal sur la terre' is met with a verbal shrug: 'Qu'importe [...] qu'il y ait du mal ou du bien?' (30:77-79). The familiar Voltairean image of providence and of a human condition subject to the will of an inscrutable and indifferent deity, whose awareness of man's suffering is comparable to the sultan's with regard to the mice in the hold of one of his ships, now reappears. Final causes, the origin of evil, the nature of the soul, the mysteries of pre-established harmony, are fathomable only by 'Sa Hautesse' (30:79-81). Pangloss asks what is to be done, and is told simply to keep quiet. As Pangloss is incapable of stemming the flow of Leibnizio-Wolffianisms, the dervish slams the door in his face, and on his jargon. The dervish's point about the futility of 'raisonnements' is stressed further through narrative event with the news of further impalings in Constantinople. The dervish's 'te taire' lingers on in the text with Martin's deferment to Candide and conversion to a philosophy of silent action: 'Travaillons sans raisonner' (30:133).

A longer conversation scene, whose perfect structure reflects the harmony it is meant to suggest, takes place with the unheroic Turkish farmer, another *bon vieillard* trope, radiating contentment as he sits beneath his orange trees, impervious to the horrific backdrop.When Pangloss asks about the identity of the executed *muphti* and *vizirs*, the farmer's ignorance of events in Constantinople arises from conscious, 'Eldoradan' disengagement from, rather than negative indifference to, the phenomena of 'partial evils'. Acceptance that not all problems are solvable is not weakness, but wisdom: 'mais je ne m'informe jamais de ce qu'on fait à Constantinople; je me contente d'y envoyer vendre les fruits du jardin que je cultive' (30:100-02). Such a strategy might well be a coded message commending caution to the embattled *philosophes*, as some critics have suggested (e.g. *16*, p.111-12), although in the years of public campaigning against injustice and judicial violence after *Candide* Voltaire did not follow such advice.

While a sumptuous meal is being served, and Candide, Pangloss and Martin are having their beards perfumed by the daughters of 'ce bon musulman', Candide learns that the farmer cultivates his twenty acres with his children, and that work on his farm has had three beneficial consequences:

boredom, vice and need have been eliminated (30:112-13). Happiness is now firmly linked to the work ethic, and to the notion of cultivation. The revisionist view is that as a solution to the problems of the human condition, as Voltaire has portrayed it, work is a banal and entirely inappropriate response (*41*). Work can never be a solution to the irresolvable, of course, but it can ensure a measure of survival and dignity (*24*, pp.48-49). Allusions to gardens and their cultivation are woven almost symphonically into the text of Chapter 30, a refrain whose notes were first heard at the start of the Eldoradan interlude (17:39-40). In Chapter 30 there are five references in all, the last two, both in response to Pangloss, articulated by Candide as imperative calls to duty requiring the abandonment of abstractions.

Candide thinks deeply about the conversation with the farmer (30:114-15), and his conviction that the latter's situation seems infinitely preferable to that of the six kings prompts Pangloss to launch into a long, superfluous enumeration of the dangers of power, only to be interrupted in mid-sentence by Candide (30:129). The interruption in the flow of learned references (*7*, p.259) marks the moment of reversal in their relationship. Moral and intellectual authority now lies with Candide, and for the first time Pangloss accepts that Candide is right (30:129-30). His association of Candide's project with the biblical account of man's role as a worker in the Garden of Eden before the Fall closes a circle of biblical allusions opened at the start of Chapter 2: 'Vous avez raison, [...] car quand l'homme fut mis dans le jardin d'Eden, il y fut mis *ut operaretur eum*, pour qu'il travaillât' (30:133-34; cf. Genesis, 2.15).

The allusion to Adam's garden also alerts the reader to the broader implications of Candide's call to action, and in particular to the question of man's responsibility for his own destiny. Work, the punishment for Adam's sin, will offer man a different kind of salvation in Candide's garden. Candide's use of the possessive should be noted. The individual pursuit of happiness has become a collective enterprise, but without the cost to individuality hinted at in Eldorado. The pursuit of happiness has changed from being a solitary activity to being a shared enterprise achievable only in terms of co-operative endeavours. Even Martin now sees a glimmer of hope: 'c'est le seul moyen de rendre la vie supportable' (30:133-34).

Revisionist critics of *Candide* argue that Candide has learned nothing, and that the *conte* has culminated in a meaningless, bathetic impasse (e.g. *23; 41*). Others have seen in Candide's garden an opening of possibilities rather than a closing. Candide and his companions form 'la petite société', and agree to participate in the 'louable dessein' (30:135) to which each is able to contribute his or her unique talents. Perceptions change, and transform a situation that seemed hopeless into one of hope, self-perception being inextricably linked to self-determination.

The Old Woman's balance-sheet is redrawn, and debits (30:15-30) now become credits. Work is no longer a curse, but an emancipation in which each character plays to his or her talents, recalling another biblical parable (Matthew, 25): Cunégonde's ugliness is tempered by the fact that her cakes are excellent, fulfilling the early promise of her 'appétissante' nature in Chapter 1 in an unexpected way. Paquette is a good seamstress, and the Old Woman excels in the laundry. Cacambo has already demonstrated his linguistic and problem-solving skills, and Giroflée can make furniture, 'et même devint honnête homme' (30:137-40). The practical use to which the two philosophers can be put is less clear (*13*, p.99-100), although the episode with Jacques showed that even Optimists can have their uses. Pangloss is good at mathematics, and might do the accounts. Martin, who once worked in the book-trade, also has useful skills. Candide has a military experience that has already been put to use, having killed three times in the course of his adventures, leaving aside the cool slaughter of monkeys. We can assume that the defence of the garden will be in safe hands. Each character is defined in the end by his or her productive capacity.

Given its geographical position on a narrow strip of land, outside the city, with the open sea on two sides, and the Straits of the Bosphorus on a third, the garden is well-placed for both defence and, if necessary, escape. The final location of Candide and his friends in Turkey, not known in the eighteenth century as the safest place on earth, has affinities with Voltaire's own 'île suisse', where he saw himself as 'un vieux Turc'. The impaled heads in Constantinople are worrying, but the violence appears to be self-contained – at least for the moment (there are no guarantees in this world). Candide's garden is no Westphalian castle, nor is it an Eldoradan hideaway, cultivating but not marketing its fruits. The Turkish evils are under observation, their monitored realities well understood by the observers.

So is all for the best? Pangloss continues to thinks so, even if the best of all possible worlds that he now perceives is no longer that of Thunder-ten-Tronckh. He is unaware of the implications for the Leibnizian notion of the *plenum* of his concession that the best of all possible worlds is not a fixed, but a moveable feast, and that a 'perfect' world can after all be exchanged for an even better one created by human effort rather than divine will. The discredited chain of cause and effect is unravelled for the last time as he traces the origins of Candide's garden back to the Baron's kick (30:143-49).

Pangloss, however, is not allowed to have the last word, or to derail with further heady speculation the dynamic nature of the enterprise that Candide has set in train. Voltaire leaves his hero engaged in a world of action, solidarity and collective human endeavour and aspiration. Pangloss might be right in a way; events might be 'enchaînés', but the chain of cause and effect has been finally reduced to events in a *conte*, its application to the world of the reader explicitly denied. Optimism has become literally *fiction*, an imaginative construct that must now be discarded if the task in hand is to be accomplished: 'Cela est bien dit [...] mais il faut cultiver notre jardin' (30:150-51). When words fail, there is a garden to be worked.

This is no conventional happy ending, just a modest affirmation of a future with no guarantees, or even foreseeable shape to it, in which survival can never be anything more than a conditional possibility. The last lines of the *Poème sur le désastre de Lisbonne* were built around the word *espérance*. At the end of *Candide* hope is at most an inference, and Voltaire is much more explicit on the need for action. In this we must look for guidance, not to kings or gods or even philosophers, but to ourselves, and to other human beings, because without them we are alone. Man is embarked and his fate, like Providence itself, is unknowable. God is not denied in *Candide*, but He is silent and inscrutable, leaving the men-mice in the hold of the cosmic ship to get on with their lives. Happiness for the little society is a secular, demythologised experience. The great questions posed during the course of events are left suspended in the air. For some the tale's conclusion might be uncomfortable and incomplete, aesthetically and philo-sophically disappointing perhaps. Responding pragmatically to the problems of the present, Candide's garden answers some basic human needs: having a full belly, work to do, and the support, co-operation and consolation of friends. As for the future, Candide has nothing definite to offer other than participation in an act of faith in the realisation of man's potential in a world in which everything is possible, but nothing certain. To those who would like to go further than that, and offer grander, more sublime visions, Candide advises silence, and Voltaire laughter.

8. Postscript: An Old Woman's Tale

Candide's reiterated, minimalist response to Pangloss at the end of the tale opens up more questions than it answers, and perhaps this is as it should be in a great work of art capable of fascinating generations of readers with its timeless vision of a world that remains only too painfully recognisable. Our attention focuses naturally on the meaning(s) of that well-trailed, resonant, but ultimately elusive, formula *il faut cultiver notre jardin* with which Voltaire chose to leave his reader. However, this should not be to the exclusion of other elements in Chapter 30 that inform its context and enlarge its meaning. Pangloss's and Martin's final positions, for example, should also be carefully weighed in any interpretation of the mosaic of *Candide*'s conclusion. Nor should the contribution of the Old Woman be overlooked, her function as one of Candide's interlocutors, here as elsewhere in the tale, being especially significant.

Candide's cautious, less eye-catching reaction to the Old Woman's formulation of the unresolved dilemma of what happens next, 'C'est une grande question' (30:44-45), is not a casual aside but a luminous response that does not invite the reader to disregard her long statement. The Old Woman's role in the last two chapters is substantial, and strengthens the view that what she says and represents has a more significant bearing on the meaning of *Candide*'s final scenario than might be assumed. It should be recalled, moreover, that in terms of her overall presence in the *conte*, she has the longest tale to tell, and that hers is the only subplot whose intrusion into the narrative is convincingly motivated.

Candide's exhortation to silence and gardening draws as deeply on her wisdom and experience as it does on other beacons of light. In the portrayal of this mysterious, mutilated figure Voltaire encapsulates the experience of suffering on many levels, and offers a richly summative image of that central tableau at the heart of *Candide*, namely a humanity at bay before the forces that seek its destruction. Her story is that of a life-force enriching the meaning of the tale's conclusion as much, if not more, than that of any other single character, apart from Candide himself.

She made her first appearance at the end of Chapter 6 just after Candide had been 'prêché, fessé, absous et béni' at the *auto-da-fé* in Lisbon. She takes his hand and tells him in Messiah-like tones to take heart and follow her (6:36-38). She soothes his wounds, feeds him, and shelters him. Her acts of *bienfaisance* save Candide's life, her curative powers making him feel so much better that the next day he can walk a quarter of a mile to an isolated house where she reunites him with Cunégonde (7:1-34), still attractive at this stage, thereby enabling the hero to experience a rare moment when the dream of love is allowed to become real. The Old Woman is the only character, other than Candide (eventually) and Cacambo (intermittently), who shapes events, facilitating and precipitating action and change. In Chapter 9, after the murder of Don Issacar and the Grand Inquisitor, it is she who provides the horses, and makes the arrangements for Candide's escape from Cadiz (9:36-49).

The events in her life, recounted during the voyage to the New World (Chapters 11-12), are soberly related at a sustained level of harrowing detail: the poisoning of her young husband, Prince Massa-Carrara, her capture and rape by pirates, her mother's dismemberment in the Moroccan bloodbath, her enslavement in Algeria, and her experience of the siege of Azof in the Russo-Turkish war where she lost her left buttock in the cause of a starving city. A life of unrelenting misery, poverty and pain leads her to the brink of suicide, 'mais j'aimais encore la vie' (12:95-96). Suicide, in many ways a rational option, and obliquely hinted at here and in the incipient nihilism of the second paragraph of Chapter 30, is firmly rejected. She ends up as one of Don Issacar's servants, and Cunégonde's companion in degradation.

The story of the Old Woman is used by Voltaire to dramatise the omnipresence of moral, physical and meta-physical evil in a creation from which God is absent. Her story mirrors Voltaire's view of a humanity lost in a hostile, pitiless cosmos, always subject to the arbitrary workings of nature, history and chance. Using devices of recapitulation, repetition and accumulation, Voltaire structures the Old Woman's story in a way that emphasises the recurring pattern of evil phenomena, as well as their shocking banality and universality. While Cunégonde's story is ultimately that of an Optimist, the Old Woman's is that of a pragmatist whose experience of the world transcends temporal and geographical boundaries, and reinforces the tale's mythic qualities: 'j'ai de l'expérience, je connais le monde' (12:113-14).

It is with her unblinkered 'old-wives-tale' honesty of vision that, in Voltaire's view, man must arm himself if the challenge of a lethal, duplicitous world is to be met. She implies surprisingly, but significantly, that her life-story is not a matter of great consequence. She would not have bothered to tell it at all, had she not been provoked by Cunégonde, and had there been any other way of relieving the tedium of a long sea-voyage. Her tale, within a Chinese box of other tales, is presented as part of a game for the amusement of the passengers: 'Donnez-vous un plaisir: engagez chaque passager à vous conter son histoire' (12:114-15). She gives no explanation or rationalisation for what has happened to her. In her story a human life has no meaning beyond the immediacy of experience. She lives in the present, and for the present. The meaning of her past, like that of the world itself, is impenetrable, and therefore not a subject for serious contemplation. Her tale, and her special way of telling it, suggest that all life-stories are part of that hideous chaos of existence that passes for the best of all possible worlds, but that life itself is still precious in spite of the odds. Survival *against* the odds is the only game that matters. This is the game that must be played, not the game of philosophy *about* the odds, which simply locks man into the *huis clos* of a Baron's foolish, fragile castle. Evil is abroad in the world, but the Old Woman shows that submission and defeat do not necessarily follow. Nowhere else in *Candide*, in terms of narrative event and characterisation, is the Optimism of the 'happy madmen vho [*sic*] say that all what is, is well' (D7931) so seriously and radically undermined, and nowhere else is the spirit of the conclusion more clearly anticipated.

The Old Woman ensures that Candide survives in body and spirit at times when all seems lost. She demonstrates the efficacy of stoic resilience, and the sheer tenaciousness of the human will under pressure. She shows him what it means to be human, and (literally) how to be free. The garden to be cultivated is purchased in response to her intimations of 'une meilleure destinée' (29:19), and what Candide will do with his garden emerges from her assessment of the alternatives. The Old Woman's *continuing* tale, sharpening, refracting, embellishing, enriching and mythologising so much of *Candide*, does more than just illuminate the conclusion. It helps to transform Voltaire's 'plaisanterie d'écolier' (D8119) into what Jean Sareil has rightly called 'une libération' (*31*, p.104).

Select Bibliography

COLLECTIVE WORKS AND CORRESPONDENCE

1. *Œuvres complètes/Complete Works*, ed. U. Kölving *et al* (Oxford, The Voltaire Foundation, 1968-). This new critical edition is still in progress, but see *7*.
2. *Œuvres complètes*, ed. L. Moland (Paris, Garnier, 1877-85). Still the standard collective edition pending the completion of *1*.
3. *Correspondence and Related Documents*, ed. T. Besterman. The second, definitive Besterman edition. See *1*, Volumes 85-135 (1968-77).

EDITIONS

The following editions of *Candide* contain particularly useful introductory essays, notes and other critical apparatus:
4. *Candide*, ed. J.H. Brumfitt (Oxford, OUP, 1971). Still a very useful edition with an informative introduction.
5. *Candide, ou l'optimisme*, ed. A. Magnan (Paris, PUF, 1987). Clear, incisive introduction, concentrating on formal aspects of narrative.
6. *Candide, ou l'optimisme*, ed. A. Morize (Paris, Didier, 1957). This is the second edition by Morize, and still an indispensable source of information in spite of being overtaken by more recent scholarship.
7. *Candide, ou l'optimisme*, ed. R. Pomeau. See *1*, Volume 48 (1980).
8. *Candide*, ed. H.T. Mason (London, Bristol Classical Press, 1995). This latest edition contains a very full and informative introduction, and reproduces *in facsimile* the text from the last authorised edition of Voltaire's works, the 1775 'encadrée'.
9. *Candide, ou l'optimisme*, ed. C. Thacker (Geneva, Droz, 1968). Contains a particularly thoughtful and stimulating commentary on themes and sources.

STUDIES

SVEC = *Studies on Voltaire and the Eighteenth Century*

10. P.-L. Assoun, 'La querelle de l'optimisme dans *Candide* et ses enjeux philosophiques', see *18*, pp.26-46. Closely and lucidly argued analysis of the debate on evil and optimism as reflected in the structure of *Candide*.

11. W.H. Barber, *Voltaire: Candide* (London, Arnold, 1960). Contains a concise account of the genesis and philosophical background.

12. Y. Belaval, 'L'esprit de Voltaire', *SVEC*, XXIV (1963), pp.139-54).

13. C.J. Betts, 'Exploring Narrative Structures in *Candide*', *SVEC*, CCCXIV (1993), pp.3-130. A fruitful application of a modified structuralist approach to the formal qualities of the text.

14. —. 'On the Beginning and Ending of *Candide*', *Modern Language Review*, LXXX (1985), pp.283-92. An illuminating analysis of the parallels between Westphalia and Candide's garden.

15. J.-P. Bigel, '*Candide*: du château au jardin', see *18*, pp.65-71. Offers a useful analysis of individual chapters, including a good explanation of the revisions to Chapter 22.

16. W.F. Bottiglia, *Voltaire's Candide*. In *SVEC*, VIIA (1964). A comprehensive, book-length, positivist account of the themes.

17. D.I. Dalnekoff, 'The Meaning of Eldorado: Utopia and Satire in *Candide*', *SVEC*, CXXVII (1974), pp.41-59. Presents Voltaire's utopia as satire rather than as model.

18. J.P. Fenaux (ed.) *et al*, *Analyses et réflexions sur Candide* (Paris, Ellipses, 1982).

19. R. Gardes, 'L'Univers religieux de *Candide*', see *18*, pp.124-31.

20. P. Henry, 'Sacred and Profane Gardens in *Candide*', *SVEC*, CLXXVI (1979), pp.133-52. A well-conceived analysis of a central feature of the text.

21. R.J. Howells, 'Cette boucherie héroïque: *Candide* as Carnival', *Modern Language Review*, LXXX (1985), pp.293-303. A successful application of the Bakhtinian critical approach.

22. —. *Disabled Powers. A Reading of Voltaire's Contes* (Amsterdam, Rodopi, 1993). A stimulating reading of Voltaire's tales in the light of Bakhtin's concept of the carnivalesque.

23. D. Langdon, 'On the Meanings of the Conclusion of *Candide*', *SVEC*, CCXXXVIII (1985), pp.397-432. A sceptical view of Candide's garden as a positive outcome.

24. H.T. Mason, *Candide. Optimism Demolished* (New York, Twayne, 1992). A well-written and well-informed study, particularly good on characters and plot, plus a detailed and balanced discussion of alternative interpretations of the conclusion.

25. —. *Voltaire* (London, Hutchinson, 1975). See particularly pp.57-73 on *Candide*, and pp.83-85 on Voltaire's treatment of the *conte* format.

26. C. Mervaud, 'Du carnaval au carnavalesque: l'épisode vénitien de *Candide*' in *Le Siècle de Voltaire: Hommage à René Pomeau*, ed. C. Mervaud and S. Menant (Oxford, The Voltaire Foundation, 1986), vol. 2, pp.651-62. An original and illuminating interpretation of the Venetian scenes.

27. G. Murray, *Voltaire's Candide: The Protean Gardener*. In *SVEC*, LXIX (1970). A book-length study linking *Candide* to the letters that Voltaire wrote at the time of composition.

28. V. Mylne, 'Literary Techniques and Methods in Voltaire's *contes philosophiques*', *SVEC*, LVII (1967), pp.1055-80. A clear and helpful overview of Voltaire's narrative practices.

29. R. Pearson, *The Fables of Reason. A Study of Voltaire's Contes Philosophiques* (Oxford, Clarendon Press, 1993). This is an important study for an understanding of Voltaire's techniques of demystification. See particularly Chapter 8 on 'The Candid *Conte*', (pp.110-36).

30. R. Pomeau, 'Candide entre Marx and Freud', *SVEC*, LXXXXIX (1972), pp.1305-23. Looks perceptively at Voltaire's treatment of work and sex.

31. J. Sareil, *Essai sur Candide* (Geneva, Droz, 1967). A brilliant interpretative study marking a post-war watershed in *Candide* criticism.

32. C. Sherman, *Reading Voltaire's Contes: A Semiotics of Philosophical Narration* (Chapel Hill, University of North Carolina Press, 1985). A useful semiotic analysis of discourse and narrative. See Chapter 3 on *Candide*.

33. J. Starobinski, 'Le fusil à deux coups de Voltaire', *Revue de métaphysique et de morale*, LXXI (1966), pp.277-91.

34. —. 'Sur le style philosophique de *Candide*', *Comparative Literature*, XXVIII (1976), pp.193-200. A short, but brilliant, study of ironic structures and style.

35. H. Stavan, 'Are Voltaire's Tales Narrative Fantasies?', *SVEC*, CCXV (1982), pp.281-87. A reply to Wolper (*41*).

36. P. Stewart, 'Holding the Mirror up to Fiction: Generic Parody in *Candide*', *French Studies*, XXXIII (1979), pp.411-19.

37. C. Thacker, 'Son of Candide', *SVEC*, LVIII (1967), pp.1515-31. A survey of the eighteenth-century imitations.

38. J. Van Den Heuvel, *Voltaire dans ses contes. De Micromégas à L'Ingénu* (Paris, Colin, 1967). A comprehensive treatment of themes. See particularly pp.236-91.

39. I. Wade, *Voltaire and Candide. A Study in the Fusion of Art, History and Philosophy* (New Jersey, Princeton University Press, 1966). Excellent account of the genesis of the tale in the light of Wade's discovery of the La Vallière manuscript (which is reproduced in facsimile).

40. J. Weightman, 'The Quality of *Candide*', in *Candide, or Optimism*, ed. R.M. Adams (New York, Norton, 1966), pp.151-64. A penetrating look at the tone and style of the narrative.

41. R.S. Wolper, 'Candide: Gull in the Garden?', *Eighteenth-Century Studies*, III (1969-70), pp.265-77. An important revisionist article on the 'message' of *Candide*, concentrating particularly on a reading of the last chapter.

CRITICAL GUIDES TO FRENCH TEXTS

edited by
Roger Little, Wolfgang van Emden, David Williams